THE
MYSTERIOUS
EPIGENOME

THE
MYSTERIOUS
EPIGENOME

What Lies Beyond DNA

THOMAS E. WOODWARD
JAMES P. GILLS

Kregel
Publications

Library of Congress Cataloging-in-Publication Data
Woodward, Tom.
    The mysterious epigenome : what lies beyond DNA / Thomas E. Woodward, James P. Gills.
        p.   cm.
    Includes bibliographical references
1. Human genetics—Religious aspects—Christianity. 2. Medical genetics—Religious aspects—Christianity. 3. Intelligent design (Teleology) 4. Apologetics. I. Gills, James P., 1934- II. Title.
BL255.W66   2012   231.7'652—dc23   2011038829

ISBN: 978-0-8254-4192-9

CONTENTS

Contents

INTRODUCTION: BEYOND DNA

THE NEW FRONTIER. Those words rang out in political speeches during the campaign season of 1960 as a youthful presidential candidate began to stir the nation with a vision of courage and initiative, a vision of un-tapped possibilities and beckoning adventure. John F. Kennedy struck a rhetorical chord and the phrase resonated widely. Historians rou-tinely refer to President Kennedy's administration as The New Frontier. After Kennedy's inauguration, the idea of a "new frontier" seemed to be widely embraced across the political spectrum. Its spirit transcended party politics. At its root, it captured a much broader narrative of our facing and seizing the challenges that loomed on the horizon.

On April 12, 1961, just eighty-three days after Kennedy took office, one of America's greatest scientific challenges burst onto the world scene when Russian cosmonaut Yuri Gagarin successfully orbited the earth in a spacecraft. The Russians, who had been "first in space" with their launch of the Sputnik satellite in October 1957, had now scored another spectacular first. Over the next six weeks, President Kennedy worked closely with NASA officials to draw up a comprehensive plan for expanded space exploration by the United States. This master plan was presented to a joint session of Congress on May 25, 1961. In one of his more memorable lines, the president said, "I believe that this nation should commit itself to achieving the goal, before this decade is out, of landing a man on the moon and returning him safely to the earth."[1]

That goal was reached in July 1969, when Neil Armstrong jumped from the ladder of the lunar module and landed on the dusty surface of the Sea of Tranquility. In the years since that historic milestone, the United States has tackled many other frontiers of science and technology. One of the most ambitious and promising projects was the Human Genome Project, launched in 1990, which aimed to map the entire human genome, right down to the exact sequence of adenine, thymine, cytosine, and guanine along the double helix. This herculean task—somewhat analogous to the goal of landing on the moon—took nearly a decade of labor by thousands of scientists and the expenditure of billions of dollars.

The first major goal was reached in 2000, when President Clinton called a news conference to announce that a rough draft of the genome had been assembled. After a few more years of refining and cross-checking the data, the project was completed in 2003 and a final draft of the genome was published. At last, scientists had delivered a complete map of our human DNA—right down to the positioning of tens of thousands of genes on the different chromosomes. Thanks to the coordinated efforts of geneticists around the globe, anyone could directly access online the exact spelling of the entire 3.1-billion-letter DNA database for *Homo sapiens.*

By most standards of scientific discovery, this project was a magnificent success. However, some of the practical promise of this project remains unfulfilled. For example, there has been little progress in the so-called gene therapies anticipated in the days when the project was being organized. As the headline of a recent front page article in the *New York Times* announced, "A Decade Later, Genetic Map Yields Few New Cures."

In the article, writer Nicholas Wade expresses disappointment that "medicine has yet to see any large part of the promised benefits. For biologists, the genome has yielded one insightful surprise after another.

But the primary goal of the $3 billion Human Genome Project—to ferret out the genetic roots of common diseases like cancer and Alzheimer's and then generate treatments—remains largely elusive. Indeed, after ten years of effort, geneticists are almost back to square one in knowing where to look for the roots of common disease."

The Human Genome Project was an undeniable success in advancing our knowledge of the programming of the DNA hard drive, but its payout in terms of *health-enhancing strategies* seems to have fallen far short of the expectations raised in the early 1990s. How could this be? Is not the human genome a prime example of a new frontier that has been faced and conquered? How could this achievement produce such minimal results in terms of medical breakthroughs?

Spelling out the encyclopedic text of our DNA is indeed a major scientific achievement. Yet perhaps what has been missing, at least in connection with human health, is an equally important genome-related frontier—one that lies *beyond* DNA and is just now coming into focus.

In probing the operation of DNA, scientists have learned much more about a second biological encyclopedia of information that resides above the primary information stored within our DNA. Researchers have discovered a complex system in the cell—sophisticated "software" situated beyond DNA—that directs DNA's functions and is responsible for our embryonic development and the differentiation of a single, fertilized egg cell into more than two hundred cell types in a mature body. This higher control system is also implicated in aging processes, cancer, and many other diseases. It guides the expression of DNA, telling different kinds of cells to use different genes, and to use them in the precise ways that meet the needs of those different cells. This "information beyond DNA" plays a crucial role in each of our sixty trillion cells, telling the genes exactly when, where, and how they are to be expressed. Welcome to biology's mysterious new frontier—the *epigenome*.

How could this huge key to the function of DNA remain hidden for so long? President Kennedy once said, "The greater our knowledge increases, the more our ignorance unfolds." This truth applies just as powerfully to the world of biology and genome research as it does to physics or political theory. In any academic field, scholars are continually poking and probing into the obscure corners of the unknown; in doing so, they not only find out new truth, they also realize how much ignorance they harbored before the search began. In the case of DNA's depths of complexity, each discovery seems to raise fresh questions and new opportunities to see *what we don't know.*

In *The Mysterious Epigenome*, we shall focus our study on two revolutionary arenas. First, we will explain the latest news in the world of DNA, which is curled up like a chemically encoded hard drive in the nucleus of all plant and animal cells. Each month, it seems, brings yet another remarkable discovery of the unexpected richness of information embedded in DNA. We find these discoveries too exciting and too important not to share.

Second, interwoven with the stories of these recent DNA discoveries, we will recount how science has stumbled onto the master control system that sits above our genetic riches. We will describe the nooks and crannies of the wondrous epigenome that is now being diligently mapped and cataloged. Much of this system resides very close to our genes; it is dynamically connected to the double helix in the form of a multilayered system of tiny chemical tags. Thus, the term *epigenome* commonly refers to these control tags that are in close relationship with DNA. Yet, in our journey through the epigenome, we will use the word in a slightly broader sense. We will include all layers and levels of cell memory and stored information found beyond the DNA.

Picture the genome of DNA as a sailing ship sitting in calm waters, tied up to a dock, ready for a journey. When the winds arise, the captain wants to venture out to sea, so he wisely sets the sails to catch the wind and moves the rudder to direct the ship to its destination. In our analogy, then, the captain, sails, and rudder are the multilayer epigenome. We want to explore and understand every part of this biological "ship-at-sea," including the all-important DNA and every dimension of the cell's epigenetic programming that directs the expression of DNA.

We have chosen to emphasize the theme of human health, especially in relation to discoveries of the epigenome. Undoubtedly, the most exciting aspect of this explosion of epigenetic information is the potential for our proactive role in reprogramming our epigenome—to some extent at least—to allow for improved health for everyone. As we'll see, some aspects of this epigenetic improvement can even be passed on to future generations.

We have spent several years studying the new revolutionary picture of the genome and epigenome emerging from lab research. The deeper we penetrated into this realm, the more we sensed the time was ripe for a guided tour of both of these frontiers of biology. Our interest and qualifications for writing on this topic are linked to our work as research scientists and science writers, with specialties in ophthalmology and scientific rhetoric and argumentation. We previously collaborated on the book *Darwinism Under the Microscope*, and have also individually published other science books.

Our hope for you, the reader, is that this book will be but the start of an awe-inspiring journey, exploring the wonders of our cell's beckoning frontier. Let's take the plunge into our genome, our epigenome . . . and beyond!

CHAPTER ONE

SCIENCE'S SUPREME QUEST

Unlocking Our Master Codes

DNA, THE MASTER CODE OF LIFE, is flashing an impish smile. She has been a bit coy and evasive recently. Now we know why. She's been harboring some shocking scientific secrets.

During the past two decades, this delicate, spiral molecule has played a game of genetic hide-and-seek with scientists. Fortunately, she has whispered some helpful hints, and scattered clues on the fingerlike landscape of her chromosomes. One by one, those clues have started to fall into place. One can almost glimpse her nodding in delight as her sequestered mysteries are pried open.

Researchers have been stunned by many of these findings. One is the discovery of a sophisticated "splicing code" found embedded within the familiar DNA code. This set of instructions enables a single gene to perform the feat of knitting together a bewildering variety of different gene products—numbering in the hundreds and even thousands. It is like a brilliant chef producing a single "super recipe" from whose instructions cooks can produce three thousand different sumptuous dishes.

Another shock came in June 2007 when the ENCODE project, a combined effort of dozens of laboratories, turned up something totally unexpected. Previously, vast stretches of the human genome had been described as "junk DNA," based on the belief that 90 percent or more of our genetic sequences were sheer, useless gibberish. According to this pre-2007 view, these junky stretches of DNA (unlike functional genes) were not being opened up and translated into RNA copies. If this vast quantity of junk DNA were graded in terms of its vital function, it would receive an F. It was seen as useless debris—damaged goods that accumulated during long eons of evolution.

The ENCODE study, however, showed that this picture was radically false. The exact opposite conclusion about so-called junk DNA has now been substantiated. Those stretches of humble DNA are anything but junky. Much of their mysterious code is in fact being read and copied, and it is used in a wide variety of cellular functions. As scientists begin to grasp the vital functions of this genetic black box, much is yet to be learned. However, one thing is certain: the credibility of the junk DNA doctrine has been heavily damaged, almost certainly beyond repair, and textbooks are being rewritten to accommodate this surprising reversal.

A LIFE-CODE ... BEYOND DNA?

One of the key DNA discoveries concerns a mysteriously intertwined "dance partner" in the elegant waltz of cellular life. The discovery of this chemical partner presents mind-boggling implications for our physical health and spiritual well-being. In a nutshell, we have now learned that our DNA responds to cues from a higher control system written into the cell, and the programming of this system can even change over time. Thus, our own healthy (or not-so-healthy) life habits can affect the way DNA is processed in our cells.

This may come as a surprise, because our DNA library, the genome, has been viewed as an ironclad inheritance for each of us. Thankfully, that's not the end of the story. Scientific sleuths have uncovered a sophisticated genetic control system, which they call the *epigenome*. We can think of it as a molecular computer code that has been lurking quietly inside living cells—*beyond our DNA*.

This built-in director, found in all of our cells, sits above our DNA and carefully controls how genes are expressed. This has been compared to a skilled musical director waving a baton in front of an orchestra. This remarkable system actually has several layers, or levels, that all seem to be tightly coordinated into one smooth system. Let's sketch a few of the key discoveries that have been confirmed as scientists plumbed the depths of the epigenome.

First, if one envisions the epigenome's role as the orchestra director of DNA, this is a director with metaphorical "eyes and ears." This biochemical conductor is sensitive to his biological environment. The quality of his directing can be changed as he picks up signals that tell him what is happening in the body's tissues and organs. For example, he can be strengthened in his daily work with a sensible diet, which supports his efficient DNA-directing, or he can be damaged and poisoned through binging, which leads to sloppy and even fatal waving of his wand. In fact, it appears a myriad of life habits can either strengthen or damage the DNA director. We will return to this in a moment.

Second, we've learned much about the clever mechanics that enable this system to work so efficiently. The director's functions are intricately woven together in a chemical software program, with its own set of codes composed of tiny signals and switches. At the heart of our book (between pages 80 and 81), we've placed detailed color images to show how these chemical signals might appear if we could see them directly through a nanoscale microscope. (We will refer to these images by letter throughout.)

Two of these epigenetic codes are embedded very close to the DNA in a double-tiered library of instructions—a database that governs the DNA-library hard drive. This dual-library differs from cell type to cell type, so that a brain cell's epigenome would be noticeably different from a muscle cell's epigenome. In the same way, both of these epigenetic libraries are different from those programmed into each of the other two hundred or so cell types. If we could zoom in on the intricate nooks of DNA's molecular landscape, we would see millions

Table 1.1. Genetics vs. Epigenetics		
Field of Study	Genetics	Epigenetics (Epigenomics)
Complete Library	Genome	Epigenome
Function	Codes for RNA & Proteins	Controls DNA Expression
Informational Format	DNA Language (in genes)	(1) Methyl tags on C-letters (2) Tagging of histone tails
Variation from Cell Type to Cell Type	None: the genome is identical in all cell types	Much variation: 200+ cell types, so 200+ epigenomes
Heritable Changes	Yes: mutations in germ cells are inherited	Yes: epigenetic modification can be passed on to successive generations
Changes by Lifestyle	No	Yes—many ways

of these chemical switches. Some epigenetic signals are hard to spot—they're very tiny and are written onto the double helix itself. A second epigenetic code involves five different markers, which are attached to the spools (called "histones") that DNA is coiled onto (see color images, figure A). Scientists have a name for this coiled-up DNA material: *chromatin*. This "packaged DNA," which makes up the stuff of our chromosomes and is buried deep inside the nucleus, is a prime focus of epigenetic research.

Moreover, several lines of evidence suggest that additional layers of subtly coded information are built into other parts of the cell, including the cell membrane and even the interior structural members of a cell. This strange new realm of functional information, written into parts of our cells that are distant from DNA, can be startling when one hears of it for the first time. It's a bit like discovering that the digital memory in a computer is not confined to the hard drive, but that millions of bits of vital data are inscribed in other specialized languages and codes which are embedded in the keyboard, screen, outer casing, and many other parts of the computer.

Just as this higher "control library" has been dubbed the *epigenome*, the study of this complex system is called *epigenomics* or, more commonly, *epigenetics*. (See table 1.1, which compares genetics with epigenetics.) A growing network of researchers is probing the mysteries of the epigenome, and the complexity of the system they're unraveling seems to grow with each passing month.

REPROGRAMMING FAMILY HEALTH FOR GENERATIONS

Perhaps the most sobering discovery that has emerged from this research is that crucial changes in a person's epigenetic code *can be inherited by succeeding generations.* In other words, scientists have found that our system of epigenetic control is not only modified and re-edited by our lifestyle, but these changes can also be locked in to some extent; they can be passed down to our children, and even to our grandchildren and perhaps beyond. One fascinating study was published by Dr. Lars Bygren of the Karolinska Institute, a highly regarded research facility in Stockholm. Bygren focused on the health histories of ninety-nine families in a tiny village in a remote agricultural region called Norrbotten in the northernmost part of Sweden.

As Bygren studied the life patterns in this village, where his own father grew up, he uncovered a stark reality. A pattern of binge-eating in years of abundant harvests seemed to have dealt a devastating blow that lasted for many decades, as it reprogrammed the epigenetic system of young boys in the village. By studying the patterns of diet and longevity in these lineages, Bygren concluded that an average of thirty-two years were cut from the life spans of the next two generations of farmers because of a single year of gluttony.

This research, originally reported in prestigious science journals, was laid out starkly in a January 2010 *Time* magazine cover story, titled "Why Your DNA Isn't Your Destiny," that surveyed the explosion of epigenetics research.[1]

The potential for influencing the efficiency of one's own DNA function—and especially for reshaping the health prospects of succeeding generations—is clearly headline news in the world of science. Yet it is much more than that. These discoveries have brought us to the edge of a scientific revolution in the biology of inheritance. Several lines of evidence, summarized in various books and research articles, have shown that many patterns of daily living—including diet, stress, smoking, and exercise—have the power to partially reprogram our epigenetic system and that of our offspring. How widespread is the fruit of such epigenetic changes (for good or ill) in the generations that follow? How many generations can reap the effects of these epigenetic alterations? Answers thus far are sketchy, though this is the focus of much current research. One thing is clear: *our epigenome is somewhat malleable and moldable.* We can tweak our epigenetic code, which then may produce either a positive or negative effect on our posterity as tiny chemical markers are modified. Several lines of evidence are delivering an epigenetic shock: the quality of our grandchildren's lives may be influenced by the way we live our lives today. As John Cloud concludes in the *Time* magazine article, "It will take geneticists and ethicists many years to work out all the implications, but be assured: the age of epigenetics has arrived."

Of course, scientists have not downgraded the role of DNA or genetics in the day-to-day workings of cells. In one sense, DNA is still king; it is just as central to life today as it's always been. The library of DNA still plays a key role in ruling or shepherding the process of growth of a single fertilized cell into a gigantic sequoia, a mighty blue whale, or a healthy adult human. What is emerging today in molecular studies of genetics is a dual focus. First, we must track the intricate toiling of DNA in its ruling or shepherding process. Second, we must also track the higher control system, the epigenome—*which acts as the ruler and shepherd of the DNA*. Scientists will continue to probe the incredible genome, even as they explore and come to understand the mysterious epigenome.

It bears repeating: Because epigenetic inheritance weaves such deep changes in life and health, which does not easily happen in DNA itself, this new double focus in biology is opening a huge window of opportunity for improved human health for generations to come.

THE RIDDLES OF DNA

Over the past decade, based on an explosion of new data, scientists have had to revise their most basic notions of the double helix. Much of what was taught as fact about DNA in biology classes a few years ago has now been tossed into history's dustbin of discarded myths.

A radically revised picture of life is now taking shape. We glimpse a panorama far richer and more complex than the simple sketch in-

herited from the biological revolution that roared to life in 1953. That's when DNA pioneers James Watson and Francis Crick announced they had uncovered the elegant double-helix structure.

Since then, nearly six decades of feverish research into DNA have passed, during which time Watson and Crick continued to play

James Watson and Francis Crick, codiscoverers of DNA's double-helix structure.

key roles. Watson even helped launch the Human Genome Project in the early 1990s, which by 2000 had produced a complete draft of all 3.1 billion letters in the miniaturized DNA hard drive found in human cells.

Until 2007, scientists assumed that only 3 percent of our DNA contained recognizable genes. These genes serve as digital files (construction templates or recipes) for assembling the complex protein molecules that do most of the work in our cells. It was commonly asserted that more than 90 percent of human DNA, devoid of gene patterns for proteins, was flawed or useless. But because it seemed to do little harm, it was passed along through the generations. This mysterious and disparaged DNA was described as "junk DNA."

Stainless steel DNA sculpture that Watson donated to Clare College at Cambridge University. It sits in a field not far from the Cavendish Laboratory where Watson and Crick made their discovery.

Then the shock. By mid-June 2007, a global project called ENCODE had completed an extensive exploration of the human genome and published 28 papers, which outlined a pattern of DNA activity that was entirely unexpected. Far from describing a genome "jammed with junk," the study showed that between 74 percent and 93 percent of the DNA spiral-ladder in human cells seems to be opened up routinely in our cells. It is read and then copied into the half-ladder RNA format.

Many of these mysterious RNA molecules—including some quite tiny ones—spring into action and are used in a variety of vital functions. The news summary released by the National Institutes of Health said, "The findings challenge the traditional view of our genetic blueprint as a tidy collection of independent genes, pointing instead to a complex network in which genes, along with regulatory elements and other types of DNA sequences that do not code for proteins, interact in overlapping ways not yet fully understood."[2] One scientist focusing on the collapse of the "junk DNA" model estimated that our human genome may contain as many as 450,000 RNA genes—a vast, lurking load of DNA information that was virtually invisible a few years ago.

OUR GOAL: TO PROBE AND QUESTION

Our purpose in writing *The Mysterious Epigenome* is to recount the discoveries that have opened up a transformed picture of our genome and its crucial companion, the epigenome. In a clear and accessible way, we will survey the nuts and bolts of these systems. As we sketch a picture of this molecular landscape, we will highlight recent findings about DNA, and we'll show how the epigenome's switches and gadgets work with the help of complex machinery.

To complete this tour of discovery, we will take the reader on a fictional field trip to a high-tech cellular display, along with a pair of trips into the cell using a miniaturized exploration sub. With the help of a bit of "frame-shifting technology," submarines will zip right into the cell and visit its spherical DNA-packed nucleus. These journeys are portrayed in the setting of a new biological research laboratory in Chicago. Although this lab and its scientists are fictitious, they are inspired by the very real Biologic Institute, a research facility near Seattle, Washington. In fact, we can assure you that the scientific information in these sections is as accurate as a geneticist's lab report.

Because we are dealing with such foundational discoveries, we decided to ask the relevant "So what?" questions throughout the book. First, what is the practical impact of these new truths on our physical health and way of life? How can we live life to the fullest while ensuring that our lifestyle promotes not only our own wellness but also that of family members who will inherit our epigenetic code? Because of the urgency of these questions, we devote space to the emerging picture of the health and fitness implications of the epigenome.

Equally important—ultimately more important by far—is the question of how these findings affect our spiritual health. How does the new breathtakingly complex view of the genome/epigenome system affect our view of origins? After reviewing the newest scientific evidence, we will ask *what* or *who* designed this massive multilevel system. It would be a simple failure of nerve if we did not delve into the design implications that flow from this scientific vista. How do these discoveries reopen old questions about whether life is "designed with a purpose in mind"? If a highly integrated system of complex information is at the root of our marvelous gifts of intelligence, creativity, and love, the idea of purpose simply cannot be ignored. Because this kind of question moves into the smoke-filled terrain of the debate between Darwinism and intelligent design, such scientific questions and controversies not only excite the mind but also have the potential to arouse our emotions.

DARWIN OR DESIGN?

Because of this built-in emotional factor, we approach with special care the issue of how cellular complexity arose. This area can be difficult because for many people, Darwin and Darwinism have come to symbolize such cherished values as scientific enlightenment, critical reasoning, and educational progress. The moment one sets forth deep empirical problems with Darwinian theory (which we do at times), one risks being instantly dismissed or marginalized. Even some leading evangelical Christians have argued that we should make peace with the Darwinian scenario of life's development. They claim that the evidence for Darwinian evolution is solid.[3] Yet is this claim plausible? Can a proclamation of the "triumph of Darwin" stand in light of the experimental evidence set forth in such works as *The Edge of Evolution* by biologist Michael Behe or *Signature in the Cell* by philosopher of science Stephen Meyer? We think not.

These developments, and many more, have posed a deep and formidable challenge to Darwinian theory. More scientists than ever, not only in the Americas but also in Europe and Asia, are asking if it is plausible that mindless, undirected processes of nature were responsible for building all of the cell's high-tech hardware and its *software codes* as well. This is precisely what Darwinism claims to have shown, and those claims are now under enormous stress from the weight of new data. Using Darwin's own words, is it possible that evolutionary theory will be found "not fit to survive" the onslaught of evidence? Is the handiwork of a brilliant designer now on display for all to see?

Darwin himself had no way to glimpse the tiny machines and digital libraries that modern science has uncovered in the past century of biochemistry. He and his contemporaries viewed the cell as a fairly simple substance. (See the sidebar, "Darwin's Limitations.") But when one fast-forwards from Darwin's day to the twenty-first century, there is a drastic change in perspective. In recent years, as biologists and geneticists have worked in concert to penetrate the mysterious intricacies of the cell, phrases such as "staggering complexity" and "infinite complexity" have appeared in the literature.[4] The unexpectedly sophisticated nano-world that has opened in front of them has greeted scientists with shocking discoveries. DNA is more information-rich than we imagined—and it is tethered to an overarching high-tech software system.

In recent years, a cascade of evidence has put stress on cherished assumptions. It has raised exciting new questions about the origin of cellular complexity. What is nature saying to us all? Let's take a look.

DARWIN'S LIMITATIONS

Let's note an irony about Darwin's monumental *Origin of Species*, published more than 150 years ago. Darwin's book, brilliantly argued and clearly revolutionary for its time, was nevertheless hamstrung with a blurred and simplistic view of the complexity of life. Today, when researchers question the adequacy of Darwinian theory, with its great emphasis on the role of natural selection in explaining the rise of complexity, they are asking the hard questions. Instead of asking simply, "What did Darwin discover about the development of life?" they are also now asking, "What didn't Darwin know about the basic structures of life's complexity that we now have to face?"

Charles Darwin

Armed with an inquisitive, brilliant mind, Darwin was nevertheless hampered by inferior instruments for observing life under the microscope. As a result, when viewing a cell, he and his colleagues concluded that it was a relatively simple object. One of his contemporaries, Ernst Haeckel (1834–1919), an eminent German embryologist and devout Darwinist, agreed with this assessment. He called the cell a "simple little lump of albuminous combination of carbon"[5]—in other words, just a tiny sac of gray, biological goo. These conclusions caused Darwin and scientists of his day to misunderstand the cell's significance. Instead of understanding it as the horrendously complex building block of all life forms, they saw the cell as a simple entity, and felt free to attribute to it purely material factors.

DISCUSSION QUESTIONS

1. Since the 1970s scientists have been describing the genome as containing much "junk DNA" within its chromosomes. Then the results of the ENCODE project were published. What surprising discovery was made known about "junk DNA"?

2. What are some of the everyday analogies that have been used to compare the relationship of DNA (the genome) with the epigenome?

3. What does it mean when it is said that "the epigenome has eyes and ears"?

4. Imagine that you can compare the genome, and also the epigenome, from two different types of cells—say, a nerve cell and muscle cell. Would you expect the two genome libraries to be identical? How about the two epigenomes—would you expect them to be identical?

5. What surprising discoveries did Dr. Bygren make about the epigenome, as he looked back into the history of the genetics of farm families in northern Sweden?

6. Referring to table 1.1, where genetics and epigenetics are compared, what contrasts between the two systems surprised you the most?

CHAPTER TWO

WHAT BIOLOGISTS KNOW ABOUT DNA

(And Darwin Didn't)

SEVERAL DOZEN ADULTS AND TEENAGERS gathered in the spacious, wood-paneled lobby of a new scientific research facility on the northwest side of Chicago. Flanked by large oak trees, the two-story, modern building presented a handsome façade of beige stone, punctured with pairs of dark tinted windows. Between the building and a winding suburban road sat a small crescent-shaped pond. A crisp breeze stirred a pile of leaves huddled by a dark gray concrete sign lettered in brushed aluminum: Institute for the Study of Biological Design.

The institute had become famous for its unique approach to biological research. On the one hand, the facility was typical in many ways. Its scientists conducted dozens of experiments, prying into the hidden recesses of living cells, uncovering the details of exquisitely complex systems. What made it unique (and controversial) was that its fourteen research scientists made no secret of their strong sympathies with intelligent design theory.

Media coverage of the grand opening two years earlier had triggered some positive responses from sympathetic Chicagoans, along with negative comments from two local biology professors. One article on the ribbon-cutting quoted a biochemist from a nearby college, who declared: "Intelligent design is not science!" The reporter counterbalanced that jab with a puzzling quote from a local physics professor, who was also an avowed agnostic: "Modern intelligent design theory is actually on pretty solid scientific grounds, and has some good arguments, but I'm taking a wait-and-see attitude as to the existence of a cosmic designer."[1] A local columnist tried to discredit the institute by suggesting that a biological think tank using intelligent design theory was like NASA hiring astrologers to work alongside its astronomers. He suggested the public call the institute the "God Lab." That nickname didn't stick. Another reporter, who found the name Institute for the Study of Biological Design too cumbersome, dubbed the lab "ISBiD." Surprisingly, the name caught on immediately and was used by everyone, including the institute's scientists.

The lobby of ISBiD, with its circle of overstuffed leather couches, was a refuge from the brisk, chilly Saturday morning outside. On one side of the lobby, a gas fireplace contributed a cheery flicker of light and a welcome token of warmth. A dozen local college students, all taking an introductory Biology and Ecology course, chatted with their bearded professor. Opposite the glass entryway was the double-door entrance to a bowl-shaped auditorium. Above the doors was a brass sign: *The Incredible Cell.*

The auditorium doors opened and a tall man in a white lab coat strode into the lobby, sporting close-cropped black hair and wire-rimmed glasses. He smiled warmly and announced, "Greetings to all of you, and welcome to ISBiD. I'm Dr. Curt Grantham, one of the staff scientists here. It's a pleasure to welcome you today to our new exhibit and multimedia program, 'Journey into the Incredible Cell.' You all will be the first group to experience our new electronically animated model of the nucleus. Follow me!" He disappeared through the doors, and the group quickly followed.

+ + +

Ten minutes later, as Dr. Grantham concluded his introductory briefing, he gestured toward a tall, closed curtain behind him, and added, "In just a few minutes, we'll open the curtain and you'll be treated to a visual electronic feast. You will see a precisely accurate 3-D scale model of a human cell, which fills the equivalent of one-half of a high school gymnasium. After we point out the main components, we'll welcome you up onto the stage, and you can explore our cell model up close. Along the way, I'll involve you in some quiz questions. I'll also be glad to take your questions, so write down anything you want to ask.

"First, to prep you for the up-close tour inside our cell, we'll invite you to meet some animatronic models of a bacterium called *E. coli*. These guys live happily inside our intestines—by the billions—and do us a great service, helping us in our digestion. Come and see!"

As the group moved up to the front of the stage, a switch was thrown, opening a narrow trap door and triggering a motor, which raised into view a glass tank resembling an oversized aquarium. Inside, five battery-driven models of *E. coli* floated gently in the water, like a school of exotic fish taking a nap.

"These high-tech models have been crafted to portray the shape and dimensions of these famous bacteria," Grantham said. "Keep this in mind: the actual size of *E. coli* is two-millionths of a meter, so at our model's size, this is what they would look like if you could shrink yourself by a factor of a hundred thousand and do a close-up inspection."

One of the students spoke up, "What are those long hairs sprouting from one end of the cell models?"

"Well, let's see if we can get them in motion first." Grantham clicked a remote control switch and the long hairs began to wiggle and twirl. In a few seconds, the hairs were rapidly rotating like long, thread-like propellers. "Those long rotating whips are amazing machines. Each one is called a *flagellum* and is machine-driven down at its base in the cell membrane. In fact, each flagellum possesses a complex rotary engine that powers it. So these are essentially miniature outboard motors, complete with rotors, stators, bushings, universal joint, drive shaft, and propeller. Together, they propel the *E. coli* through liquid like a tiny submarine. You are looking at one of the great wonders of microbiology."

As the group moved closer to the tank, they noticed that the bacteria models, which had previously resembled oversized cucumbers floating in a bathtub, had now taken on a new look with their multiple propellers twirling. They looked more like hungry fish, cruising around the tank on the prowl for food. Grantham added, "Each flagellum of these creatures involves about forty parts, with each part having its precise structure encoded in digital form in forty separate genes. Speaking of genes, even bacterial cells need lots of digital information to run all of their chemical factories. It's incredible how much digital information is programmed along the spine of this tiny critter's DNA." (See color images, figure B.)

He walked over and pointed to a three-foot row of books lined up on the desk beside the tank. "Here we have over two dozen average size books—a few novels by Nobel Laureate Toni Morrison, J.R.R. Tolkien's *Lord of the Rings* trilogy, and twenty published novels of Stephen King. In their sheer content of individual letters, these twenty-five books contain the same total of letters that are packed into one *E. coli* cell: about 4.5 million pairs. If you think of this database in terms of computer files on a hard drive, that comes to 4.5 megabytes of information in this tiny critter, with over four thousand files. Now, compare that to the human genome's size—nearly a thousand times larger. The human genome has a bit over 3.1 *billion* letter-pairs—the equivalent of about 14,000 books of 250 pages each! Now, look carefully above the tank."

He pressed a button behind the tank and something like a Fourth of July fireworks display flashed in the empty space above the tank, complete with accompanying sound effects. Several psychedelic sprays of colored sparks exploded, over and over, until one massive explosion of sparks began to swirl crazily in a vibrating whirlpool of color, which then converged into a single holographic image of an elongated, bluish-hued cell.

One of the college students said, "Cool! A 3-D hologram!"

Grantham smiled, "In fact, you are looking at the newest experimental type of holography. Watch carefully."

The large cell, seemingly hovering in midair above the tank, grew in size until it was slightly larger than the tank, and the fine texture of its exterior surface came into view. In seconds, the cell membrane disappeared, and the crowded cell interior was opened to view. The moving hologram revealed complex structures that resembled a 3-D maze of thick cables and tubes stretching out in every direction. Visible in the center of the maze was a large, thick loop. As the zooming effect of the hologram continued, the loop grew in size, and the students could see that the loop was made of carefully woven threads of DNA, coiled up like hundreds of tiny kinks in a rope.

"We invite you to take a deep breath," Grantham announced. "Try to get your mind around an emerging picture of cellular complexity. We will first zoom in on the genetic library, which is composed entirely of DNA. Does anyone know what term biologists use for the DNA library found in every living cell?"

A blond teenager raised her hand and ventured, "Is it the *genome*?"

"That's right! You've probably read or heard about the Human Genome Project. As it turns out, every creature—whether microbe, plant, or animal—that has ever lived on earth has possessed a unique genome, and has been totally dependent on this storehouse of precisely written instructions."

The hologram of the bacterial loop of DNA was now so enlarged that the individual rungs in the spiral ladder were plainly visible. "You can now see the familiar twisting ladder structure of the strands of DNA," Grantham continued. "But there is one major difference in the way it is packaged. Bacterial DNA isn't packed into a spherical *nucleus*. It's woven together carefully in the shape of a loop."

The animation cruised around the edge of the loop of DNA and moved in to one spot in the double helix, so that the individual rungs of the ladder became visible. "Notice that each of these DNA ladder rungs is formed from a pair of chemical letters. When we call these units *letters*, we're not just using a crude analogy. This is how biologists describe it. DNA is not just *like* a code; DNA *is* a code. Now look carefully at the hologram."

As the bacteria's DNA helix grew ever larger in size, a single colorful stretch of rungs came into view. The dimensions resembled an oversized household stepladder. "We compare the four-letter alphabet of the DNA language with the twenty-six letters of the English alphabet, or the thirty-two letters in the Cyrillic alphabet used in Russia. The four letters in DNA's alphabet are A, T, C, and G. Sometimes, scientists call these four letters the four *bases*. A single rung in the twisting ladder of DNA has two paired DNA letters, so it is said to contain a *base pair*. This model you're looking at has twenty rungs, so how many base pairs does it have?" (See color images, figure C.)[2]

After a slight pause, several students blurted out, "Twenty!"

"Bingo!" said Grantham. "Look carefully at the holographic animation and you'll see that A, T, C, and G are the first letters of the names of the chemicals. Maybe some of you had to memorize these names in school. *A* stands for adenine, *T* for thymine, *C* for cytosine, and *G* for guanine. Now I want to show you our little memory trick for recalling the four letters and their pairing system. As I turn off the hologram, look up toward the ceiling."

He pushed a button on the console and from high up in the ceiling a twisting-ladder plastic DNA model, some forty feet in length, was lowered by a trio of narrow aluminum arms until it was suspended ten feet above the stage. With a flick of another control switch, roughly half of the colored rungs in the DNA ladder began to glow like Christmas bulbs—in bright colors of red and green—thanks to embedded miniature LED lights.

"In our DNA models, we use a color code that makes it easy to remember the letters. We symbolize *C* using the color *crimson*—another word for red. The letter G is pictured by the color *green*. Just as crimson and green go together—you can think of them as the Christmas colors—so C and G always go together in DNA."

A second switch turned off the C–G lighted rungs, and seconds later, the remaining ladder rungs on the model began to glow brightly in combinations of orange and blue.

"Now you can see the other pairs of letters, the A–T letters, which also have colors linked to them. We had to get creative here. The DNA letter A is represented by *azure*, another word for blue. For comparison, the Spanish word for blue is *azul*. The letter that is always paired with A is T, which we picture by the color *tangerine*, which of course is a synonym for orange. So, the A–T pairing of letters in DNA is shown by letter duos of azure and tangerine. If it helps, you can think of them as the colors of the Gators—the University of Florida."

One student raised his hand and added, "My dad went to Auburn and I think that those are also Auburn's colors."

"True—and they're also the colors of the Universities of Illinois and Virginia, and they're complementary colors on the color wheel. Now, it's time to light up our entire DNA model."

All of the helix's ladder rungs began to glow, showing off the gorgeous crimson–green and azure–tangerine pairings. As the double helix started spinning slowly, a recording of soft music began playing and a female narrator said, "You're now looking at the world's largest model of a single human gene."

The narration paused as the crimson–green DNA rungs began to flash in an alternating sequence with the azure–tangerine rungs. In sync with the strobe-like flashing of the colored rungs, an energetic melody of synthesized music sprang to life. As the visitors took in the view of the strangely colored twisting necklace, the taped narration continued: "With 450 color-coded rungs in our forty-foot DNA ladder, this model actually represents one of the shortest genes in the human genome."

DNA, SUPERSTAR

DNA: is it as famous as a superstar? Perhaps. You are probably familiar with the use of DNA by the FBI and other law enforcement agencies to identify the guilt or innocence of alleged criminals. DNA can discern the truth of past events, but it is also famous as a predictor of the future. Samples taken from a fetus are analyzed in order to detect or predict genetic diseases.

DNA's superstar status is sometimes carried to an extreme. Some evolutionary theorists elevate DNA almost to the level of an all-powerful (if unconscious) deity, controlling our every move. One who has nearly deified DNA is Richard Dawkins, the evolutionary biologist who has become an evangelist for atheism. In *River Out of Eden*, he writes: "The universe we observe has precisely the properties we should expect if there is, at bottom, no design, no purpose, no evil, and no good, nothing but blind, pitiless indifference. . . . DNA neither cares nor knows. DNA just is. And we dance to its music."

But by Dawkins's view, can we then be truly free to explore the truth about ourselves, the universe, or God? Or by this view, would not our beliefs be mere mirages served up to us by our DNA puppet-masters, as we "dance to its music"? In other words, how can evolutionary biology itself, as a belief that is part of DNA's dance that we perform, escape this self-refuting view of reality?

Another aspect of DNA is superstar-famous: the iconic image of DNA's double helix in the form of a twisting ladder. For a visual aid to illustrate DNA's intricacies, we encourage you to watch the acclaimed documentary "Unlocking the Mystery of Life," by Illustra Media. The DVD, now in twenty-six languages, features brilliant 3-D computer graphics of DNA and the other long-chain molecules—RNA and proteins. Superb special effects show the construction of a protein chain with the help of a ribosome machine (which we will encounter in chapter 3). (For pictures of the macromolecules from this film, see color images, figures E and F.)

One "sweet way" to build a DNA model at home or school is to employ colored gumdrops for the four letters.[3] The C–G letter pairs are shown by crimson gumdrops paired with green ones; A–T pairs are shown by deep azure gumdrops paired with tangerine ones. To complete the connecting DNA side chains, use marshmallows: large ones for DNA sugars, and small ones for the phosphates. All are connected together with toothpicks.

The music faded and Grantham explained that, for better visibility, the gene model had been enlarged to a much greater degree than the cell model. "In fact," he added, "our model was magnified an extra thousand times in size beyond the enlargement scale of the cell. Now, you may wonder how many genes—programmed sections of DNA—inhabit any given cell. For example, how many genes does our bacterial friend *E. coli* have? Since humans have more than twenty thousand genes, it may surprise you that *E. coli* has more than four thousand distinct genes—4,288 to be exact.

"Genes can be thought of as unique little booklets—or you can think of them as important files on a computer. They are housed in the genome, and yet these four-thousand-plus genes of *E. coli*, so vital in carrying out the huge number of functions of the cell, are so tightly condensed, they fit into a space ten thousand times smaller than the period at the end of this sentence. Scientists have concluded that no entity in the known universe stores and processes information as efficiently as the DNA molecule.

"Now, in a moment we'll take a look at how DNA functions in a living cell. The double helix reigns as the superstar of all the molecules that inhabit a cell. Yet DNA doesn't work alone. It depends on two other partners, which are also long-chain macromolecules. Does anyone here know what the other two are called?"

A teen ventured, "Are the other two the RNA and protein molecules?"

"Right—and that makes the audience three for three in answering my quiz questions. I think it's time to reward you, so you all are invited to enjoy a complimentary beverage of your choice at our café before you leave. It's on us—I can personally recommend our cappuccino."

Grantham continued, "What I've described as the three *long-chain molecules*—the *DNA, RNA,* and *proteins*—are sometimes called the three *macromolecules,* because they typically contain many hundreds, or even tens of thousands, of chemical letters linked together in each chain. Now, before I show you what DNA's two partners look like, let's stop and take a question or two."

Spotting the professor, he said, "Yes, sir—you're the one I briefly spoke to earlier—was it Dan?"

"Yes, I'm Dan Ross, and I teach biology at Westlake College just down the road. Two questions: I've read conflicting reports about how much 'junk DNA' is in our genome. Can you share an update? And second, I understand that our genome is not the largest animal genome, right? Don't some animal and plant species have even more DNA in their cells than we do?"

"If you can hold on to that first question," said Grantham, "let me cover the issue of *junk DNA* later when we enter the cell model. On the other question—it is certainly true that the size of the human genome is dwarfed by other species. Many plants have higher quantities of DNA, per cell, than what we find in the human genome. This phenomenon is sometimes called the 'C-value Paradox' or the 'C-value Enigma,' where the C-value relates to a measure of the gross quantity of DNA in a cell, which doesn't necessarily correlate to the level of complexity of that species. For example, a Japanese plant, *Paris japonica,* holds the plant DNA record at 149 billion letters per cell. [See color images, figure G.] Even a species of wheat has nearly sixteen billion letters per cell—that's more than *five times* as much DNA as we find in each human cell. So that should give you some extra respect for your next slice of bread, since it was made from wheat cells whose genome puts ours to shame—at least in sheer size.

"Human genomes are also comparatively modest in size compared to many species in the animal kingdom. Many salamander and newt species have genomes that are gargantuan—from 10 billion up to 120 billion letters of DNA per cell—and the marbled lungfish has 140 billion letters per cell! Perhaps strangest of all, the record-holders for 'DNA quantity per cell' are totally unexpected. Who would have thought that first and second place would be held by a pair of lowly single-cell species—*Amoeba proteus*, which has 290 billion letters, and the incredible *Polychaos dubium*, which harbors about 670 billion letters of DNA. To put this in perspective, we can say that humble *Polychaos dubium*, which hardly grows bigger than a poppy seed, is comparable to a laptop computer with a 670 gigabyte hard drive, or an iPod programmed with 20,000 songs. Now, are there any more questions?"

A young woman near the back raised her hand. "I'd like to know what Darwin knew about all of this. Even though he didn't know about DNA itself, he knew about genes, right?"

"Actually, Darwin had no knowledge of the kind of biological complexity we're talking about here," said Grantham. "In fact, he knew literally nothing about the details of the genetic inheritance carried within cells—not even Mendel's momentous discovery of dominant and recessive genes. Some scientists and historians have noted his ignorance of basic concepts of genetics. I would suggest that his lack of knowledge, in itself, does not deliver any sort of verdict on his theory. Yet it certainly paved the way for his development of a theory of nature-driven incremental change. In Darwin's mind, any new body structure could be developed step-by-infinitesimal-step, over long eons of time. So his ignorance of cellular complexity was certainly formative, in one sense. It contributed to a rejection of a highly reasonable explanation for life's digital complexity—namely, *intelligence*—and it opened the door to a simple materialistic explanation—the idea that nature's unguided and unintelligent forces were the sole cause that shaped the world of biology, including its system of inheritance."[4]

Grantham paused for a moment. "If there are no more questions, it's time to open up what you've been waiting for: The Incredible Cell."

He reached down, pushed a button, and glanced behind him as silent motors opened the tall curtains, revealing something strange, almost surreal and otherworldly, in appearance. The audience gasped as the lushly decorated, oversized model of the interior of a living cell was revealed—a huge, reddish cavern, whose walls curved like the interior of a bubble. Its surface was slightly undulated, as if the ripples in a scarlet pond had been suddenly frozen in place. The walls, ceiling, and floor were populated by all sorts of strangely shaped objects. Majestic orchestral music began to flow and the lights were dimmed. A taped narration began, and each of the key parts of the cell was identified, one by one. As each part was named, that object was brightly illuminated by carefully aimed spotlights.

"Now," said Grantham, "the time has come to meet the other stars in DNA's trio—the RNA half-ladders, and the absolutely amazing workhorses of life, the *proteins*. Follow me now into the Incredible Cell, and I'll let you shake hands with one of these stars."

DISCUSSION QUESTIONS

1. How does DNA resemble a language that humans use every day—what is common to both?
2. How is DNA's function like that of a computer program?
3. Where is the DNA stored inside animal and plant cells? How is DNA stored differently in bacterial cells?
4. What remarkable machine does the *E. coli* bacterium possess that involves forty genes to set up and operate? What are some of the "design characteristics" of this system?
5. How is the DNA of a single *E. coli* comparable to a row of twenty-five novels?
6. How familiar with the basic ideas of genetics was Charles Darwin? Why?

Chapter Three

TWO GRAND, UNSUNG HEROES

Proteins and RNA

As the audience entered the stage, Dr. Grantham said, "I'm going to bring into view DNA's two colleagues: an RNA molecule and a protein molecule. He punched a button, and another dangling chain slowly descended from the ceiling until it was suspended next to the DNA chain. It was the same exact length, but instead of a full twisting ladder, it was a half ladder, looking somewhat like the other model, except it was cut in half right down the middle.

As soon as the RNA model was in place, other motors began to hum, and a few seconds later, a third chain of identical size came slowly into view, looking like a string of large, irregularly shaped footballs, linked together in a fifty-foot chain.

"Now you can see not only the RNA copy of the DNA, but also the protein chain that is built from the RNA blueprint. All three of the macromolecules are visible now," said Grantham.

He paused, while the group wandered under the models for a few moments, enjoying the close-up view. "As you can see, the structure of RNA is very similar to that of DNA, except it is shaped like a half ladder. In terms of its architecture, it's a DNA ladder that has been cut right down the middle. It has one simple side chain, and sticking out from that chain is a precise sequence of stubby half-rungs. Just as in DNA, these rungs contain the coded information, and each rung is formed by one letter from RNA's specialized four-letter alphabet. There's one thing that's different about RNA's alphabet. One of the letters in DNA, the T (thymine) is replaced by a chemical labeled U (uracil). So RNA's four-letter alphabet is A, which is paired with U; and C, which is paired with G. In our color-coded system, the *U* is symbolized by the color *umber*, which is a medium shade of brown."

With this, he flipped another switch and embedded lights lit up the RNA chain. A chorus of "aahs" arose from the group, as the half-rungs glowed warmly and steadily in their bright crimson, green, azure, and umber shades. After a few seconds of steady glowing, these four colors also began to blink on and off sequentially, producing another pleased murmur from the group.

"Even though DNA is more famous, we (and our cells) can be supremely thankful for RNA. We are totally dependent on the trillions upon trillions of precisely coded RNA chains in our bodies. Most famously, they act as the vital 'photocopies' of key portions of DNA. In addition, scientists are now discovering many other vital roles that RNA plays within the cell, and especially inside the nucleus. It seems that each month, a new kind of important RNA molecule is discovered. Many of them are quite tiny, yet they are extremely important.

"This is a good time to answer Dan's question about the idea of junk DNA. This older view—that much of our DNA is 'genomic junk'— prevailed in biology up until recently, because there was so much we didn't know about the DNA that seemed to be sitting there inert, doing nothing. At least, this strange DNA contained no coded genes that were used to produce proteins. Now we have learned that much of the supposed junk DNA is just the opposite of junk. A gigantic project called "ENCODE" focused on forty-four scattered target areas in the human genome, covering thirty million base pair rungs on the DNA ladder. Scientists uncovered a treasure trove of evidence for something called 'RNA genes.' This result, announced in 2007 and steadily con-firmed since then, is one of the most exciting and unanticipated areas of modern genetics."

Grantham switched off the blinking RNA lights and directed the group's attention back to the DNA model suspended from the ceiling, whose lights flashed on again. "If you were listening carefully when we looked at *E. coli* earlier, you may have caught my comment that, in most animals and plants, the double helix is normally found tightly wound into bundles within the nucleus of the cell. The nucleus—which you see above you, suspended from the ceiling in the center of the cell arena—is a spherical container whose thin wall is perforated by tiny holes, called nuclear pores. These pores are not simple holes, however; they are more like complicated, mechanized gateways, and each pore is built using at least thirty precise, machinelike parts that lock together. In a typical human cell, this spherical library compartment will have about two thousand pores scattered over its surface. Now, take a look at those pores on the nucleus—let's see if we can brighten them up a bit."

Through his remote control, Grantham made the huge nucleus be-gin to rotate, and an intense light began to shine at the center, sending tiny shafts of light out of each of the hundreds of tiny nuclear pores. The moving beams of light bathed the walls of the cell model with a swirling pattern of moving dots, making the Incredible Cell display resemble a disco dance floor.

"Let's focus again on the all-important gene in the functioning of DNA," said Grantham, drawing the group's attention once more to the suspended DNA model. "Human DNA, which is stashed in our nuclei, is laden with well over twenty thousand of these precise sequences, each one of which is a genetic file in our hard drive. A typical average-size human gene is composed of between one thousand and five thou-sand pairs of DNA letters, so our model of a gene is quite short at a mere 450 pairs. We did not show it in this model, but genes typically have what Richard Francis has called a 'control panel'—which is not part of the protein-coding sequence itself, but is rather a 'regulatory region to which proteins and other chemicals bind, either inhibiting or promoting the DNA transcription."[1] Now, watch the far end of our gene model carefully, and we'll see what happens to DNA that enables it to be read."

At one end of the gene model, the first five feet of the fifty-foot DNA ladder slowly began to open up and unwind. Through tiny, built-in motors within the helix, the suspended genetic ladder split open, like a zipper on a backpack. "Through this unwinding process," said Grantham, "the DNA letters become exposed, with the assistance of protein machinery. This then allows another team of sophisticated protein machines to swoop down on that exact predetermined spot on the DNA and begin to make a copy of the exposed information. That's where the RNA chain is assembled."

At this point, Grantham turned off the DNA's flashing-light rungs, while the RNA rungs kept blinking. "The DNA has done its job. So all the action is focused now on the RNA copy, which contains the precisely coded sequence found on the DNA. The gene's crucial information—the building plan for a protein molecule—is now safely transferred to the RNA copy. In human cells, something very strange happens next. Our RNA chains, right after they are built, typically become the target of some amazing splicing and editing activities, but that's pretty complicated stuff and I'll skip that for now. I need to spare you a possible headache from information overload."

Grantham led the group into the center of the exhibit and pointed out three large lumpy shapes, the size of old fashioned bath tubs, suspended from the ceiling behind the nucleus. Each looked like a thick, rounded loaf of bread with a bumpy surface; various grooves and deep indentations were visible on the lumpy shapes. "Now I want to introduce you to our amazing *ribosomes*. When the RNA chains are assembled, they slip out of the nucleus and are ushered over to these strange-looking ribosome machines, which perform some of the most vital and amazing work of any machine in the cell." (See color images, figure H.)

Pointing his laser beam at one of the tunnel-like indentations on the side of the suspended ribosome model, he explained, "These ribosome models are accurate representations of the master machine that builds all of the proteins in a cell. In order to build a given protein, this incredible machine uses the pattern it receives from the RNA chain that has come out of the nucleus. This is called 'messenger RNA.' If you look on the side of the ribosome, I'm pointing to the crucial tunnel where the RNA enters. This machine then takes the tiny RNA strip of information, and translates its RNA language into a new language—the protein language, which has a twenty-letter alphabet. So as the RNA is fed into the ribosome machine, it passes through it like a train through a tunnel. In the process, the RNA is read, three letters at a time, and the ribosome produces a protein chain."

Reaching for his remote control, Grantham whispered, "Let's see if we can turn on the ribosomes and get them busy producing proteins." The three ribosome models suddenly began to glow an intense purple, illuminated from lights built into their surface. "These guys are going to get busy now, so let's give them some busy-sounding music." With another click, the music from the cantina scene in *Star Wars* began to play, and from the bottom of each ribosome, a lumpy chain began to emerge. It was as if each ribosome was a plump, headless animal that had decided to rapidly grow itself a long tail. As soon as the tails began exiting the ribosome, they began to curl together, folding into a lumpy mass. When over ten feet of the twisted, folded protein tail had emerged from each machine, they were instantly detached and fell gently to the floor.

"I said earlier that you could shake hands with a protein when you came up on the stage, so feel free to go over and look at this product of the ribosome. These are accurate models of what a protein chain would look like if you could hold it in your hands!" The group swarmed over to the spots where the soft, nerf-like chains—now folded together into a lumpy mass—had fallen into a small heap on the floor. Hands reached out to touch them like an exotic furry pet.

While the visitors were inspecting the scrunched protein models, the biology professor asked, "May I make sure I'm understanding the relative size of these ribosomes? A student just asked me how big the ribosome is, and I said I thought that they were much smaller in relation to the nucleus."

Grantham nodded. "That's a good observation. I was about to say that, in relation to the nucleus, the ribosomes *are* much smaller, about twenty-billionths of a meter in size. They are so small, that at this scale you would see them, but they'd be tiny—just under a half inch in size. So we've made them over one hundred times larger than they would be—compared to the scale of our display. We did that so that you can see what their shape is like, including the RNA-reading tunnel. Even though it is small compared to a nucleus, this sophisticated machine is still pretty chunky. Its body is made of several gigantic RNA molecules, and at least fifty-three proteins. Altogether, each ribosome comprises more than 350,000 atoms! The ribosome's parts are actually built inside the nucleus; but once they're assembled outside the nucleus, the ribosome is too big to fit back through those nuclear pores. So a ribosome is just a bit larger than one of those pores."

A gray-haired woman asked, "Are there just a few of these ribosomes in a cell?"

"Oh, no . . . there are about twenty thousand of these little guys in a typical *E. coli* cell; and in some human cells—for example, liver cells—there can be a swarm of several million—even up to five or ten million of them toiling away in a single cell.

"Now, let me wind up by saying a bit more about protein production, and then we're done, except for your complimentary drink in the café. As I said, there is a translation process going on in the ribosome. The information-rich RNA chain is grabbed by the ribosome machine and is quickly read, word-by-word, and turned into a different type of information—the protein. This is a bit like converting the 'Chopsticks' melody in written music form on a sheet, turning it into the piano sounds of that simple melody picked up by your ears." On cue, background music played the familiar piano tune.

"Or think of it the way an old-fashioned cassette player reads the magnetic patterns on a tape's surface and turns them into an Elvis Presley song or a Beethoven symphony." The "Chopsticks" melody suddenly gave way to Presley's hit "Hound Dog," which blared for a few seconds and then quickly morphed into the last few bars of Beethoven's Fifth Symphony. Grantham smiled and added, "If a super short protein of fifty amino acids is the molecular equivalent of 'Chopsticks,' then the longest protein—the muscle protein called *titin*, with thirty-four thousand amino acids—is the equivalent of all nine of Beethoven's symphonies played back to back.

"In the case of a cassette, or even a CD, certain patterns recorded on a surface are turned into another beautiful language—wonderful music. In the ribosome, the product of reading the pattern of words in the RNA chain is not a flow of great music, but rather a precisely ordered chain of chemical letters that form a protein. With the help of the ribosome's sophisticated reading system, those letters are pulled in one by one and linked together. As you've seen in our model, when the last word of the RNA strip has passed through the ribosome's tunnel and has been read and translated, the protein string has been born, and it detaches from the ribosome.

"To sum up: proteins are the cell's unsung heroes. They are marvels of engineering and sophisticated design. This long-chain molecule carries a specified sequence of chemical letter-units. As I said, the protein has its own alphabet: twenty different chemical letters, to be exact. These letters in the protein language are called amino acids, and they're the building blocks of all living stuff."

At this point, Grantham moved back to the control console and pushed another switch. "The last thing we will see in our cell tour is a larger scale portrayal of what happens to the protein once it is assembled. You saw a glimpse of this already when the protein chains curled up as they came out of our ribosome models. Please look back one more time at our fifty-foot protein model."

The group moved closer to the suspended protein model and

murmured as it began to slowly fold, curl, and scrunch itself. With the help of tiny embedded motors and advanced animatronic controls, in just ten seconds, the fifty-foot chain had compacted itself into a complex shape less than five feet in diameter. The onlookers broke into spontaneous applause at the robotic display. "Thank you—I'll pass your appreciation on to our electronic engineer who built that model."

Grantham walked over and stood beneath the curled-up protein. Gesturing upward with both arms, he added, "What you've just witnessed here is crucial. Once any protein chain is assembled by the ribosome, it detaches and begins to twist and fold and bunch up into a preprogrammed three-dimensional fold.[2] A protein's 3-D shape is produced by the exact sequence of its letters—the amino acids. Depending on the precise sequence of these amino acids, proteins can fold into any one of thousands of extremely precise shapes. These shapes include a dizzying variety—from simple ring structures and tubular shapes, all the way up to my favorite—a robotic worker-protein called *kinesin*. Kinesin works hard in our cells; he actually carries massive loads on his back. His body structure is amazing. He strolls down a cellular highway using a pair of floppy appendages that look like tiny legs with feet. That just about wraps up today's tour of the Incredible Cell. Don't forget to drop by our café on the way out, and thanks for coming."

INCREDIBLE COMPLEXITY—WHERE DOES IT POINT?

In the educational encounter above, we used a little bit of imagination to convey the main points that have emerged about the three long-chain macromolecules that are packed with information. DNA, RNA, and proteins are digital masterpieces, and it's no exaggeration to say they are the superstars in a world of astonishing biological complexity.

Let's focus for a moment on the workhorse of this trio, the protein. The informational requirements of just a single protein, to enable it to fold automatically into a precise shape, are so strenuous and so detailed, that our minds cannot help but be staggered by this microscopic wonder. Now, multiply that times a thousand or even a hundred thousand, and you begin to sense the astonishing complexity of a single cell. At the same time, proteins are not like luxury options on a car; they're basic to all life functions. An incredible number of proteins play a myriad of roles in building cell structures and carrying out hundreds of chemical tasks necessary to cell function.

Now, move up to the next level, and consider the wonder of how these amazing proteins team up. Scientists have cataloged protein function, structure, and working relationships, and they have found that the average size of a team of proteins working together is six. "Lone Ranger" proteins are relatively rare. As a result of this tightly integrated complexity of hundreds of teams of proteins, we can draw a key conclusion. Evidence of design doesn't just reside at the level of a single protein, but also at the group level, where proteins are precisely matched and coordinated. This work of mapping out protein form and function in a cell led in the latter part of the 1990s to the birth of a new branch of biological science called *proteomics*.

To sum up the last two chapters, the flow of information in a cell passes from the DNA (the specific genes) into RNA copies. The RNA macromolecule is then read precisely by the ribosome machine, translating from the RNA language into the protein language. Once assembled, the protein is released by the ribosome and it then folds quickly and leaps into its vital role within the cell—typically working alongside other proteins in a tightly coordinated system.

As we prepare to shift gears, let's note what biologists say about this information flow. For decades, they have taught students to memorize a little motto to summarize this flow. One version goes like this: *DNA makes RNA makes proteins*. This can be written out as a DNA flowchart:

Earlier in this chapter, we began to flesh out the story of a recent and exciting discovery that seems to defy this motto—the finding that DNA sometimes produces RNA and the process stops there. Yet, by and large, this statement holds true as the dominant traffic pattern within all kinds of cells. The most striking thing about all three molecules is that they carry within their long chains something that "goes beyond" physics and chemistry, something we are quite familiar with: *information*. These chains are information bearing, or "informational" in nature. As we said earlier, DNA, RNA, and proteins are not just *like* a language; they *are* a language. They literally carry messages, in digital code.

On this point, we would be wise to note David Berlinski, the Princeton-trained philosopher and historian of mathematics, who has become a secular critic of Darwinism. (See color images, figure I.) He is widely known for his witty exchanges with Ben Stein during an interview in the film *Expelled*. Berlinski describes the three master molecules—DNA, RNA, and proteins—as life's three "informational macromolecules." He does not hesitate to ask embarrassing questions about the origin of this information. Is there any good evidence, he asks, that DNA and its sister molecules can be crafted by the unintelligent forces of nature, as Darwinists insist? Do experiments show that scattered, lucky DNA mutations (filtered by natural selection) can mimic intelligence so as to program these macromolecules in the first place? On these points, Berlinski says, there is literally no debate. The answer to both questions is a loud, crashing, overwhelming *no*.

We can broaden Berlinski's questions and ask simply: Can matter and energy, working with time and chance, combine in any way to program any such rich informational system with its millions of letters? Have the experimental data backed the idea that undirected, unintelligent nature has such vast creative powers? One can further extend these questions to the informational layers added by the epigenome. How can scientists account for a nature-driven origin of the cell's complexity when they stumble upon new layers of information—a whole new system of coded-language—above and beyond the cell's DNA? The epigenome beckons, and it's time to dive in.

DISCUSSION QUESTIONS

1. Compare and contrast DNA's alphabet and RNA's alphabet.
2. Ribosomes are crucial cellular machines. Helped by the construction code embedded in the messenger RNA molecule, ribosomes do the work of assembling long chain-like molecules that are the "wondrous workhorses" of a cell. What molecules are we referring to? Why does the term "workhorse" seem to fit?
3. What happens to a protein chain shortly after it starts exiting the ribosome?
4. Scientists today are in awe of the complexity of (a) a single protein, as well as (b) integrated teams or systems comprised of many proteins. Give an example of the complexity of these two levels.
5. What does Berlinski mean when he calls DNA, RNA, and proteins "informational macromolecules"? In his view, how strong is the evidence for the undirected forces of nature (mutations and selection) as an adequate explanation for the rise of DNA's digital programming?
6. Some scientists emphasize that large quantities of information—like the contents of a genome—are only observed arising from intelligent agents. If this principle (based on "universal sensory experience") holds true, then what are the implications?

Chapter Four

A VAST INFORMATIONAL ICEBERG

The Newly Emerging Picture of a Cell

To confront the central question about the origin of new information in DNA, we need to retrace the story that led us to the DNA-centered and genome-focused perspective that has dominated thinking in genetics (rightly so) for more than fifty years. Turn back the clock to an afternoon in June 2000, when a presidential press conference was held to announce that a massive milestone had been reached in the history of genetics. After a decade of laborious research, a network of scientists around the globe was nearing the end of their glorious quest. They had searched out the precise letter-by-letter text of the complete human genome—all 3.1 billion letters of our DNA. At last, a rough draft was being readied for publication, under the leadership of Francis Collins, then director of the Human Genome Project. (Collins had taken over leadership of the project in 1993 from James Watson, co-discoverer of DNA's structure. Collins retired in 2008 and went on to direct the prestigious National Institutes of Health, beginning in 2009.)

As cameras captured the golden moment, Collins stood alongside President Bill Clinton and Tony Blair, prime minister of Great Britain. Collins's team was elated that the project had been completed under cost and ahead of schedule. The Human Genome Project had been an ambitious effort, with $3 billion of funding from the U.S. government. Scientists had to navigate many technical roadblocks as they developed a complete roadmap of our genome, showing the position of tens of thousands of known genes on the forty-six human chromosomes.

Since coming to prominence as head of the Human Genome Project in 1993, Francis Collins had not hidden from the press the fascinating religious side of his personal story. In a nutshell, Collins had abandoned his atheism as a young scientist, and had become an evangelical Christian. To a large number of scientists, the "God question" is viewed as irrelevant to their work. Some, like Richard Dawkins, assert that God-belief is a dangerous delusion and is harmful to human flourishing.[1] The editors of *Time* magazine were so struck by the stark religious contrast between these two renowned scientists, they invited both to come to Time-Warner headquarters for a dialogue that evolved into a feisty "debate in print." (This was *Time*'s cover story on November 13, 2006.)

Collins's path to faith, which is sketched briefly in his book *The Language of God*, was triggered by an awkward question posed by an older patient during hospital rounds in the late 1970s. In contrast with the patient's words of firm hope in the face of a deadly illness, Collins had nothing to say when she asked about his own hope. Shaken somewhat by this question, he began his own reading program, and soon found himself enmeshed in C. S. Lewis's classic introduction to biblical faith, *Mere Christianity*. Lewis argues that one of the ways God reveals himself to us is in the "moral law" (i.e., the law of right and wrong, perceived in our conscience). Collins concluded that Lewis was right, and he started perusing the Bible. Before long, he was persuaded that the central message about Christ was true, and worthy of his trust and commitment.

At the human genome press conference in 2000, Collins did not hesitate to connect the DNA achievement with its theological meaning. For example, Collins helped write President Clinton's speech, which said, "Today we are learning the language in which God created life." Sharing his own comments, Collins said, "It is humbling and awe-inspiring to realize that we have caught the first glimpse of our own instruction book, previously known only to God."[2]

Obviously, Collins's theological views would not be shared by the vast number of biologists who are atheists—more than 90 percent of the biologists in the elite National Academies of Science, according to one survey.[3] To them, such ideas carry no scientific weight at all. The idea of DNA as a "language of God"—the phrase that became the title of Collins's 2006 book—merely expressed his own subjective (emotional, imaginative) perspective. To these atheist colleagues, such verbiage is little more than a personalized veneer or decoration that sits atop the hard scientific facts. As oratory, atheists regard such words as irrelevant to our understanding of reality, although they may be helpful to reassure the American public that faith in God had nothing to fear from tax-funded DNA research.

DIVING INTO THE INFERENCE TO DESIGN

Yet, one can frame this idea of a "language of God"—written in cells as DNA, transcribed into strips of RNA, translated into chains of proteins—as more than a pleasant metaphor, more than poetry. It is entirely possible that, from a strictly scientific perspective, the codes, languages, and information-packed libraries we see in cells are sending us a "signal of intelligence." That is, they present to us a kind of unique pattern, which, in our observations of the universe, only arises from an intelligent agent.

This idea—the ability of science to detect intelligence in nature—is the core of one of the most controversial subjects of our time: the scientific theory of intelligent design (ID). We have already written on this controversy in our earlier books.[4] The central ideas of ID are perhaps best expressed now in books such as Michael Behe's *The Edge of Evolution* (2007), William Dembski and Jonathan Wells's *Design of Life*

(2007), or Stephen Meyer's *Signature in the Cell* (2009). The ideas and discoveries that undergird design theory are communicated on the DVD documentary that caused a sensation when it aired on the Public Broadcasting System: *Unlocking the Mystery of Life.* The DVD sequels—*The Privileged Planet* and *Darwin's Dilemma*—have proved to be just as cogent, and just as controversial.

Rhetorical attacks on design theory have been harsh and at times brutal. Some opponents of ID have dismissed the theory as "creationism in a cheap tuxedo," and some intense outbursts from Darwinists have even characterized ID as a threat to America's leadership in science. Two books published by Oxford Press even indulged in indefensible hyperbole, charging ID with endangering the future of science itself, and even of Western civilization.[5]

Yet several leading scientists working in design theory have seen progress in publishing their work in peer-reviewed literature. In lab experiments especially, many recent developments bode well for ID's ongoing progress. We sense the debate has now reached a crucial turning point as fresh data on DNA mutations raise embarrassing questions about the cherished core of neo-Darwinism—the purported "engine" of selection and mutation.[6]

What many onlookers don't realize is the irony that intelligent design theory uses a guiding principle from Darwin's close friend and fellow scientist, British geologist Charles Lyell. This is the idea known as "uniformitarianism"—the somewhat controversial notion that the present is the key to the past. Put simply, those cause-and-effect relationships we see at work in the present should serve (in general) as reliable guides to figuring out the past development and change of life on earth. This rule needs to be carefully applied, of course, and it faces some important limitations.[7] Yet, as a general rule, it has stood as a scientific key to exploring the past.

Here is how ID uses the uniformitarian principle: *If, in our experience today, we only see coded language and information-packed strings of letters arise from intelligent causes, then it seems to make sense that the same effect in the past (DNA's informational digital database) arose from the same kind of cause (intelligence).*

This rule seems to hold true when applied to even a short line of text. Imagine staying as a guest in the home of friends. At 6:45 AM, just after the wife has left for work, you venture into the kitchen to see if there is any coffee. On the kitchen counter, a box of Alpha-Bits cereal has toppled and spilled its contents. Moving closer to this chaotic conglomeration, you see at the front edge a line of cereal letters: PLEASE TAKE OUT THE GARBAGE AND WALK THE DOG. Seeing this, you would legitimately (logically) infer that the wife had left a message for her later-rising husband. In fact, an "intelligent cause" seems the only straightforward, logical inference to be drawn. The alternative theory (the Chance-Spilling-of-Letters Theory) is ruled out instantly. And yet, this is just a string of thirty-six letters. How much more solidly might we infer an intelligence as being responsible for the highly organized genome of the simplest known bacterium (*Nanoarchaeum equitans*) with its genome of 490,885 DNA letters organized with precision into 552 genes?[8]

BRACE FOR A GENETIC SHOCK

Now brace yourself for a rude shock. What holds true about the "conclusion of design" (also called the "inference to design") in explaining thirty-six letters on a kitchen counter, or a half-million DNA letters in the simplest bacterial genome, would apply more strongly if the entire DNA library in plants and animals were found to be integrated with a higher level of information and control.

Let's do a thought experiment. Imagine that, one day, scientists probing ever deeper into the secrets of the cell stumble upon the realization that the DNA was simply functioning as the cell's "filing cabinet." The genome then would be seen as housing in its drawers all the necessary blueprints for building an array of machine parts. Those drawers would be absolutely vital, of course. Depending on the cell type, certain drawers would be opened with great frequency—and particular file folders would be removed, and the blueprints therein would be copied, and taken over to the machine shop. Yet, the whole process of deciding which files to open and copy, at just the right time, and the entire overarching process of coordinating multiple steps to bring about enormously complicated building and control operations—that control process is by far the higher reality. The higher informational reality (beyond the filing cabinet) is represented in our thought experiment as the mind of the construction engineer. He is the one who selectively chooses the blueprints in the filing cabinet, and he fulfills a large number of coordinated purposes. This "higher control" could prove to be the most information-packed part of the system.

Here, at the higher control-level of DNA, is where a series of scientific tremors are now being felt. In the introduction and chapter 1, we told of the great surprise of biologists as they uncovered layer upon layer of additional master control information beyond the genomic filing cabinet of DNA. We identified this store of information as the *epigenome*—a word derived by adding the Greek prefix *epi*, which has the nuance of "over" or "above," to the familiar root word *genome*. The *epi*genome refers to the entire coordinated system of "control information" that resides above and beyond the bare DNA sequences. We are seeing an explosion of research into this mysterious world of additional information that acts as the construction engineer working with the DNA filing cabinet—or, to switch metaphors, the director working with the genomic DNA orchestra.

Among the scientists we consulted about the cellular information embedded above and beyond our DNA was biologist Richard Sternberg, who was interviewed by Ben Stein in the opening of the documentary film *Expelled: No Intelligence Allowed*. Sternberg holds two earned doctorates—in evolutionary biology and in systems biology. In *Expelled*, Sternberg explained how colleagues regarded him "as a terrorist" and treated him shabbily at the Smithsonian Institute for simply following proper procedures as editor of its affiliated journal,

The Proceedings of the Biological Society of Washington (PBSW). His "scientific crime" was allowing an article submitted by design theorist Stephen Meyer to pass through the normal peer-review process, and then allowing it to be published once it was *approved* by the three peer-reviewers, none of whom were design theorists.

Since leaving the Smithsonian, Sternberg has focused his research on the genetic complexity of the cell and the new picture of the gene and genome that is emerging. He has written and lectured about the problems in the "junk DNA" hypothesis, and criticized the old "material basis" view of a gene. In relation to the epigenome, Sternberg has affirmed that, above and beyond the DNA, scientists are stumbling upon "layer upon layer upon layer" of new cellular information. In our discussions with Sternberg, we proposed the possibility of an iceberg analogy. In this picture, the layers of new epigenetic information constitute a large part of the vast hidden informational iceberg that lurks below the waterline—along with the so-called "junk DNA" that is proving to be anything but junk. On the other hand, the DNA sequences that code for proteins are the mere tip of the iceberg—the shining tip that biologists have focused on during the past four decades. Dr. Sternberg acknowledged that such an iceberg picture would capture the new scientific perspective emerging from the data of genetics and epigenetics. This picture is similar to the graphic used in a recent *Time* cover story on epigenetics, in which the genome was represented by a small dot, the size of a BB, while the epigenome was a circle more than three inches in diameter.[9]

Where exactly in the cell is all of this control information interwoven? What physical form does it take? How does it work and what are its roles? How does this new information system interact with the DNA itself? These are key questions, and they will occupy our focus in the next few chapters, as we stretch your imagination a bit. We will be taking you on a submarine adventure with a biological twist: into the busy, watery metropolis we call a living cell.

DISCUSSION QUESTIONS

1. What were the key steps in Francis Collins's journey from atheism to belief in God and acceptance of the Christian faith?

2. How do atheistic scientists view or evaluate the comments from Francis Collins about the human genome being the "language of God"?

3. Charles Lyell investigated the past using the famous uniformitarian rule: "The present is the key to the past." Design theorists have seen a logical application of this idea: "*Presently observed cause-effect patterns* serve as a key to understanding the *cause-effect patterns in the past.*" How does this apply to the origin of sequences of genetic information in DNA?

4. If the "inference to design" works logically with 490,000 DNA letters in the simplest bacterium, is it reasonable that the same inference would hold if DNA were found to be integrated with a higher multilevel control system using different codes and signals? Explain.

5. Fill in this blank: "_____ sequences that code for proteins are the mere tip of the vast informational iceberg in living cells." What similar visual analogy did *Time* magazine use?

CHAPTER FIVE

DIVING DEEP INTO THE EPIGENOME

The Methyl Code and Histone Code

To EXPERIENCE THE EXCITEMENT of a visual encounter with the strange and beautiful world of the epigenome, we invite you to go back with us to ISBiD—the biological research facility we visited in chapters 2 and 3. We are now going to take you into ISBiD's Cellular Explorations Laboratory, which recently developed a new and highly sophisticated technology called "frame shifting." In our science fiction scenario, scientists have stumbled onto a mammoth breakthrough that allows the normal frame-of-reference for a physical body (including humans) to be "down-shifted" in size up to one ten-billionth of its normal size, without losing the standard operation of the physical laws that govern those bodies. If it helps, picture the microscopic galaxy with its myriad planets with microscopic intelligent beings that twirled inside the cat's bauble ("Orion's Belt") in the blockbuster film *Men in Black*.

Through this breakthrough, we will take you on a journey into the cellular ocean that scientists are observing under their microscopes. We will walk along the sandy beaches of this real, observable molecular sea, which harbors science's unexpected pockets and layers of information—a subtle and sophisticated system that mimics the role of the construction engineer or the conductor of a vast orchestra.

+ + +

It was a day she would never forget. Julie Stein, thirty-two years old, sat in the prep room of the Frame-shift Miniaturization Lab. She reflected on the rapid series of events that led to this moment. First, the announcement of a national competition among high school science teachers, to be the first "guest passenger" on a cellular voyage. Then, the news that she was a finalist, followed by the shock that her essay and interview had landed her in the "First Alternate" slot. Then last, the call two weeks ago, saying that health issues had sidelined the winner of the competition, and that she was now in line for the trip of her life.

As she stepped up into her personal, ultra-comfortable bubble submarine, she quickly reviewed her checklist, and gave a final wave to the camera which was relaying a live video feed of her preparation to the ISBiD auditorium, where friends, family, and a handful of reporters watched her progress on a large projection screen. If all went as planned, a pair of cameras built into her sub would convey to the audience virtually the same 3-D vista of the cell's interior that she would enjoy. After a launch countdown sounded out on her headset, she closed her eyes and sensed a bit of vertigo, as if a super-fast elevator were speeding downward from the top level of a skyscraper. A shrill metallic ringing filled her ears. In less than a minute, she realized that the frame-shifting was complete and she had been shrunk to a size much tinier than the thickness of a human hair. She looked straight ahead and could see the lead sub in front of her. Her guide was Dr. Curt Grantham, the staff scientist who had prepped her for the trip. Descending in his mini-sub to her right, he radioed a reminder. "No worries on staying up with me; your sub will track with mine automatically. Remember that your control stick is for orientation, to enable you to rotate your sub and look in different directions whenever we stop."

Julie had been briefed that their placement was precisely set—a few billionths of an inch from the water-engulfed surface of a living cell. Equipped with sturdy, transparent walls, the personal sub was so tiny now that, as it approached the surface of the cell, it squeezed right through the bobbing heads and trailing fronds that made up the double-layer lipid membrane of the cell wall. After a few moments of squeezing through this dark curtain-like structure, she passed into the interior of the cell, and found herself moving down into a lattice-like maze of beams and girders. It looked as if some enormous skyscraper were under construction under the sea—as if all the interior pillars, trusses, and girders were laid bare in a vast underwater cavern.

In her headphones was a brief hiss, followed by Grantham's voice: "What you see all around you is just what it seems—the internal structural skeleton of the cell. Based on research we've done, which parallels work done around the world in other labs, some of the cell's most important epigenetic information is embedded right here—in the exact positioning of these structural girders and the precise location of their attachment to the cell membrane. This informational pattern is especially powerful in the very first cell of a new creature's life—such as the human zygote. It seems that a fertilized human embryo, as it prepares to grow into a baby, has far more information stashed away in its 3-D structure than we ever imagined."

Descending through a maze of tubular braces and beams, Julie could see that she was approaching the nucleus, the spherical storehouse of the cell's DNA. At her tiny scale, it loomed as a huge, shimmering globe, an underwater city whose surface teemed with the traffic of tiny molecules shuttling to and from its surface. As the pair of subs moved closer, she saw that the molecular blobs were passing into and out of the nucleus by means of hundreds of large circular pores that penetrated the wall of the nucleus. Grantham's sub quickly approached one of the round portals, with its tiny hairs protruding around the entrance. (See color images, figure J.) His sub slipped through, and she followed, entering the nucleus.

Arrayed before them was a crowded underwater arena—a vast warehouse with hundreds of aisles penetrating the maze of stacked loops and clumps of DNA in every direction. Grantham piloted his sub into one of the narrow aisles and Julie followed close behind. Grantham came to an abrupt stop, and using the powerful beam of his directional searchlight, he focused on a single, cylindrical spool of DNA. As Julie maneuvered closer, she found herself comparing the shape of this unexpected object with the wooden spools wrapped with thread she once saw in a sewing box. The core—that is, the spool itself—had two loops of DNA tightly wrapped around it. It looked a bit like a regular spool of thread, but on closer inspection, she noted that its shape was only roughly cylindrical. The shape seemed to be a tightly packed mass of eight small clumps of spaghetti, compacted into the shape of an odd spindle.

The radio crackled again as Grantham anticipated Julie's question. "You are now looking at one of the wonders of biology that enables DNA to be compacted so efficiently. That spool is an amazing feat of design; it's comprised of eight proteins that lock together precisely. These eight proteins are called *histones*. Each of the eight units—reminiscent of a micro clump of pasta—is a string of one hundred or so amino acids that has been precisely folded into an irregular Z-shape. Once folded, those eight histones combine like a three-dimensional jigsaw puzzle to form the spool. In human cells, millions of these eight-histone spools are produced in each cell's process of dividing, so that they are ready to be used for the new DNA to be wound onto."

As Julie marveled at this evidence of clever design for storing DNA, she noticed something odd sticking out of the spool on one side, next to the layer of DNA wound up on the exterior of the histone mass. It looked vaguely like a thin branch, or a tail. Upon closer inspection, she counted four tails sticking out from the side of the histone. (See color images, figure K.) "Are there four of these narrow tails here? At least that's what I think I'm seeing."

Grantham affirmed her observation. "It's hard to see from your vantage point, but on the other side of the spool are four other tails, projecting outward the same way as you see these four on your side."

As Julie maneuvered still closer to get a better look at the closest tail dangling from the side of the spool, she noticed a funny-looking tag attached to this tail. It reminded her of a tag on a piece of luggage, except that it looked more like a stubby twig, shaped like a tiny Y. Then she spotted more of the Y-shapes sprouting from the other tails. She also noticed that the tails seemed to be pulled away from the layers of DNA on the spool.

"What am I looking at on the side of the histone spool here?" Julie asked Grantham. "It seems like the spool has some midget-size projection, shooting off the side of its tail. It's as if there is some sort of Y-shaped twig attached to the tail—in fact there are a number of them attached to the four tails. Is this important?"

"Very good observation!" Grantham replied. "You have just spotted another key marker in the epigenome system. The little tag you spotted is called an *acetyl* molecule, and you're right. There are a number of them linked to those tails. Each acetyl is attached to a precise spot on the projecting tail of the histone spool with the help of a special protein machine that is assigned to do the decorating. Oddly enough, this particular tag is acting something like an unlocking device. When the acetyl tags are placed there, it makes it much easier for the file of DNA on that spool to be pulled off and read. On the other hand, if the acetyl tags are removed by a still different machine, then the slender histone tails snuggle up closer to the two windings of DNA that are bound up on the spool. In that case, the tail acts somewhat like a clamp, making the DNA snug and secure on its spool and much harder to be read. It's like a locking and unlocking system on a filing cabinet. There is a vast pattern of acetyl-tagged histone spools all over this DNA warehouse of the nucleus."

"So is this common? Does a typical cell nucleus have thousands of these tags placed on certain spools of DNA?"

"More like hundreds of thousands—and this pattern of acetyl tagging constitutes another vital layer of information beyond the DNA. And as I said, the job of placing the acetyl tags onto the tails—or removing them from those tails—is not simple. It involves a set of specially designed protein machines that are truly specialists: they work with acetyl tags alone. The machine that swoops down to attach the acetyl tags is called a *histone acetylase enzyme*, or HAC for short. The other machine, designed to grab and remove those tags from the tails, is called a *histone deacetylase enzyme*, or HDAC. Now, look to your right. You'll see an HDAC machine is approaching—probably to remove the acetyl tags from the spool in front of you. We're going to back away from the histone so that we don't get in its way."

As Julie could feel the automatic propulsion purr, moving them back from the DNA windings on the histone, she said, "Amazing timing!" She watched the machine, which reminded her of a tiny, irregularly shaped plastic bag swimming in a narrow channel.

"Yes—perfect timing," Grantham said. "Let's watch the HDAC in action as it performs its tricks. When we finish our tour, I'll show you a histone model in my office which has not only the acetyl tag attached, but also four other kinds of chemical tags that are also found placed on those tails."

"Four other tags besides acetyl? That's incredible!"

Just then, Julie's mini-sub seemed to hum with a low vibration, which steadily built in intensity with each passing second. Hoping all was well, she radioed Dr. Grantham and said, "What's happening? What is that vibration I'm feeling? Are we safe?"

The radio system was a hiss of static for a moment. As the vibration grew stronger and caused Julie's body to begin shaking, her worry deepened. She wondered why Grantham wasn't replying. She shouted, "Dr. Grantham, can you hear me?" No answer.

Then, a sharp command came through the speakers, "Quick! Turn your sub around—right now!"

DISCUSSION QUESTIONS

1. Passing through the space between the cell wall and the nucleus, the explorers observed the internal structure of the cell's "girders and beams." Besides their role as structural members that give shape to a cell, what other surprising role do these structures play, especially in a zygote?

2. The cell's nucleus is a fascinating part of the cell. What feature or features struck you as fascinating as the explorers entered this arena where DNA is stored?

3. The threads of DNA are not just randomly "stuffed" into a nucleus, but are well organized—both at the larger level (chromosomes) and even at the smallest level (histones). What is the job of a histone—that is, what is its role in this organizing task? What does the histone remind you of in everyday life?

4. What unique structures are projecting outward on either side of the histone complex, and what kinds of "decorations" are added to those structures?

5. Acetyl tags, when added to the spooled DNA, tend to have what kind of effect on the reading process that is vitally necessary in order to process genetic messages? What change takes place to the spool of DNA when acetyl tags are removed?

6. On a complexity scale of one to ten (one being "simple" and ten being "excruciatingly complex"), rate the complexity of the system of histone spools, with their tails, and the adding or removing of (a) acetyl tags and (b) the other four chemical markers. Is an inference to "intelligent design" warranted? How plausible is it that such a system was built under the guidance of undirected natural processes?

CHAPTER SIX

THE FIFTH LETTER OF DNA

Key to the Cancer Enigma?

ROTATING HER SUB as fast as she could, Julie Stein caught a glimpse of her guide. Dr. Grantham's sub seemed to be shaking as violently as hers, as it hovered a short distance away. Julie caught sight of Grantham's face; his gaze was fixed straight ahead. Julie could spot a look of intense concentration in his eyes. Fortunately, a broad smile broke across his face as he looked toward the other end of the narrow DNA corridor.

"You are incredibly lucky today!" he said. "We happen to be in one very active section of Chromosome 17 where a key stretch of DNA is being opened up and read. That increased vibration we felt over the past minute or so was the rumble of the big protein machines lumbering down along the stacks of DNA right there in front of us. They are unlocking and prying open the correct sections of DNA spools—we call these spool clusters the *nucleosomes*. Their goal is to gain access to the target cluster of genes that are all grouped together. Watch carefully—this could be the highlight of your voyage!"

The scene that unfolded in front of Julie was so complex, so full of frenzied motion, of strange machines scurrying around the tiny islands of DNA, that later she found it hard to describe in words. However, one sequence of action stood out clearly like an unforgettable video clip. As the genetic corridor opened wider, a team of five

DNA-manager machines entered and moved like a swarm of underwater robots, grabbing, twisting, and rapidly unwinding sections of DNA from their spooled-up position on the histones. After a burst of activity that seemed to last for a minute or more, Julie saw unfurled in front of her sub the famed DNA molecule. At first, it reminded her of very fuzzy yarn; but as she drew closer, what came into focus was the shape of a gorgeous spiral ladder. Its unique form looked pretty much as she had seen in textbook graphics, except the rungs seemed knobby and thick, as if there were almost no space between them.

Grantham piloted the pair of subs down along the spine of the DNA, and as they passed by, Julie looked more closely at the smooth surface of the pairs of DNA letters, the rungs in the twisting ladder. Aiming her spotlight at a group of rungs, she noticed something odd. Here and there, the smoothness of the DNA rung pattern was slightly marred by something sprouting out from the rung—a miniscule antenna-like appendage that resembled a baby sprout of broccoli. Staring at this oddity, she thought, "This reminds me of the tag we saw attached to some histone tails, but this time it looks more like a little spherical head with three ears. I'll have to ask Dr. Grantham what it is."

Just then, in mid-thought, Julie's radio burst to life. "I can see what you're examining with your spotlight," said Grantham. "Again, I congratulate you on your powers of observation. You are looking at a special DNA chemical marker called a *methyl tag*. This tag is a midget molecule. In its free state, as methane, it has only five atoms: one carbon and four hydrogen; the methyl group has one less hydrogen—three instead of four. So you can think of the methyl tag as a stripped-down single molecule of methane—the same gas molecule you burn by the trillions in your barbecue grill at home. In animals, this tag is chemically glued only to the letter C in the DNA alphabet. So cells will sometimes stick methyl tags onto some selected (not all) C-letters. This phenomenon was first noted in 1948; but in the past few decades, we have discovered that this pattern of tagging is absolutely vital for cell functioning." (See color images, figure L.)

As Julie stared at the tiny molecular twig attached to the DNA, Grantham added a final comment. "In fact, what we've seen here is probably the most famous layer of information beyond the DNA sequences. The methyl tagging of selected C-letters may be the most massive and mysterious of all the levels of the epigenome. Tens of millions of rungs of DNA are tagged this way. The technical name for these tagged C-letters in DNA is *methylated cytosine*."

"That's a mouthful," Julie blurted out.

"Yes—some molecular biologists have even ventured to describe the tagged Cs as if they were the 'fifth letter' of DNA. Those who have this point of view may describe the DNA alphabet as having not four letters but five: A, T, C, G, and methylated-C."

"Wait a minute!" Julie said, swinging her spotlight down along the DNA stretched out before the pair of subs. "Quick question for you. First, I've been told that when the time arrives for a cell to divide into two, the entire genome of DNA is opened up in such a way as to be duplicated—all three billion rungs of human DNA split open so that replication can take place. So the result is that an exact copy of the DNA letter sequence is produced for the new cell, right?"

Grantham replied, "Correct. I think I can see where you're headed with the question."

Julie continued, "So, along the way, all the As, Ts, Cs, and Gs are copied; that's what I've been teaching in my biology classes for ten years. But what about the methyl tags? Are they forgotten and left behind on just one strand, or are they also copied, so that those thousands or millions of methyl tags are placed in the brand new copy of the duplicate DNA?"

"Yes, as amazing as it may seem, we've learned in the past decade that the methyl tags are copied over to the same corresponding rung in the new cell's DNA. This is quite a chemical juggling act, and to handle this tricky operation, a special protein machine is assigned in the cell to carry out that task. It's called *methyltransferase*. What's still rather mysterious, and the focus of a lot of research now, is that the pattern of methyl tagging can change from cell to cell. So, while the vast pattern of methyl tags is generally passed on unchanged from the mother cell to the daughter cell, there are very important exceptions. The methyl-tag pattern definitely does change in some very important ways when you go from one basic cell type to another cell type that is fundamentally different."

Swinging the spotlight back down to the small methyl dangling from the DNA rung just below her sub, Julie puzzled, "I think I follow you, but I have one last question: What is the *purpose* of the methyl tags? You just said that a human genome has millions of methyls added."

"Some scientists have estimated about two hundred million methyl tags in a single nucleus," said Grantham.

"That's unbelievable . . . but *why* is there all of this methyl tagging of DNA going on? What's the practical good of methylation?"

"Great question!" answered Grantham. "But our air supply is getting down to the one quarter mark, so it's time to surface now. I'll answer your question back in our briefing room."

WHY AN EPIGENOME?

Our plunge into the depths of the cell's beauty and complexity is an imaginative reworking of what scientists routinely stumble upon as they pry open the secrets of the genome and the mysterious multilayer epigenome. The chief difference is that they use sophisticated techniques such as X-ray crystallography, instead of mini-subs, and they employ all sorts of computer modeling programs to construct 3-D pictures of the wonders we have described visually.

One key purpose of our graphic descriptions was to review the building blocks of the cell's amazing information processing system, which we described in chapters 2 and 3. Our other purpose was to build on that knowledge and move beyond the genome to introduce at least three levels (or types) of information markers found in the epigenome. Let's review them quickly.

(1) During the descent toward the nucleus, we noted that a certain kind of information was rooted in the *exact placement of the structural girders and skeletal members* of the cell, especially their precise spot of attachment on the cell's membrane.

(2) We highlighted the presence of dangling *acetyl tags*—microscopic molecular signals—placed on some of the tails that protrude from one end of the histone spool on which DNA is wound, and we mentioned that there are four other tags, which we'll introduce shortly.

(3) Last, we zoomed in on the molecular decorations known as *methyl tags* (shaped like tiny heads with three knobby ears), which are attached to certain DNA letters—specifically, certain cytosine or C-letters. This pervasive pattern of tags is practically the star of the epigenome in studies published thus far.

Toward the end of our trip into the cell, Dr. Grantham promised Julie that he would explain the four other kinds of tags that are attached to the histone spool, in addition to the acetyl decorations. For starters, one key histone tag is the methyl tag, which we already know about from the special C-letters of DNA that receive the same tag. At some special spots in the histone tails, there can even be two or three methyl tags attached together; such locations are said to be "dimethylated" or "trimethylated."

Here are the other three histone tags: (1) Phosphate tags—these tiny molecules, which resemble methyls but are somewhat larger, are familiar actors in biochemistry; they are used to build the side-rungs of DNA and RNA.

(2) Ubiquitin proteins—these are comparatively gigantic tags; we will describe them in more detail below.

Ubiquitin protein

(3) SUMO proteins, which are as gigantic as the ubiquitins (SUMO stands for Small Ubiquitin-like MOdifiers). Compared to the other three tags, the SUMO proteins and ubiquitin proteins are huge, chunky molecular blobs (see color images, figure M).

Ubiquitins are a well-known class of proteins that are usually attached to defective, damaged, or worn-out parts of a cell to mark them for destruction by the cell's recycling system. SUMO proteins, though similar in structure to ubiquitin proteins, are somewhat goose-shaped protein machines used to mark other proteins for various purposes. Like a gigantic sumo wrestler, the SUMO protein, along with its ubiquitin cousins, weighs hundreds of times as much as the smaller tags—methyl, acetyl, and phosphate. If you think of the histone spool as an oversized suitcase, and if the smaller tags are visualized as tiny bits of paper in different shapes attached to the suitcase's handle, then adding a SUMO tag would be like attaching a plastic toy goose to the side of the suitcase.

In addition to the three levels of information we spotted during our dive (girder placement, methyl tags on C-letters, and histone tags), the epigenome contains even more informational "nooks and crannies," which we'll explore later. During the cellular dive, one of these elements was mentioned—a mysterious but important system we call the "zygote code."

At the very end of our trip into the cell, an important question was asked after the methyl tags were spotted along the backbone of the DNA: "What is their purpose?" Why are certain C-letters tagged and not others? Let's make the question broader and even more basic: *What is the role of the epigenome system?*

The answer is not yet complete, but it is steadily coming into focus. Research on the epigenome is accelerating, and scientists around the world are delving into both the molecular structure and the functional roles of the epigenome's sections and layers. On the question of methyl tagging of C-letters along the DNA spine, the data suggest that the presence of tags (either inside the gene itself, or near one end of the gene, or in the gene's adjacent "control panel") tends to *silence that gene.* On the other hand, if no methyl tags are added to a gene (nor to the gene's control panel), then that gene is like "live ammo," ready to be used at a moment's notice. On the other hand, a methyl-tagged gene is like a patient that has been given an anesthetic to put him to sleep.

The same sort of function is sometimes seen in the tagging (or tag removal) of histone tails. Through a pattern of such tags, the tight packaging of DNA on the histone spools is either made "snug and secure" (that is, the DNA wound on the spool is "locked in place" or made hard to remove), or it is made "open" (the DNA text is ready to be unwound from the spool and read). Crucially, the disposition of the DNA is controlled by chemical signals within the tagging of the spools. Acetyl tagging tends to open the spools, whereas methyl tagging seems to close up or secure the spools (we are simplifying things a bit here). The addition of phosphate tags to the tail, and the linking of SUMO proteins (or ubiquitin proteins) to the side of the spool, also seems to affect whether the DNA is open for use or locked away securely. Sometimes, several tags work together in complicated ways on the same spool, as if they were the lines in a bar code, conveying a complex set of instructions. In other words, according to current theory, the histone tags are not just locking and opening devices; they also work as signals, switches, and triggers that connect with special protein machines that are scurrying around the packed spools of DNA. Some of these protein machines, called *chromatin regulators*, act like security agents at a storage facility. Other proteins, called *transcription factors*, open up certain selected DNA spools for usage in that particular cell.

CANCER'S UGLY SHADOW: THE ENIGMA OF METHYLATED GENES

So far, one key connection has become clear between epigenetics and a massive scourge in human health: *cancer*. Various cancers have been linked with abnormalities in the epigenome. Dr. Jean-Pierre Issa, of the M.D. Anderson Cancer Center in Houston, who has devoted several years to exploring the relationship between cancer and epigenetics, notes that epigenetic switches, which control the expression of key genes, *can be the trigger for cancerous conditions*. For example, if a given gene helps modulate proper cell division, the cell depends on that gene to prevent the out-of-control cell division that is at the heart of all cancers. If histone protein tails "hug the DNA very tightly," says Dr. Issa, "then it is hidden from view for the cell. A gene that is hidden cannot be utilized. It is the same as having a dead gene or a mutated gene. These are the kinds of things that can regulate gene expression and also become abnormal in cancer."[1]

Specifically, we now know that changes in a gene such as increased methylation (silencing) or reduced methylation (activation) can act as triggers to certain kinds of cancer. For example, *oncogenes*—normally benign genes that, when mutated or expressed at high levels, play a key role in turning a normal cell into a cancer cell—are known to be a factor in causing certain kinds of cancers.[2] In some cases, medical researchers have found that the normal silencing of such oncogenes is disturbed by faulty C-tagging of their DNA letters.

Precisely how this happens is unclear, but scientists think that some factor causes the pattern of methyl tags to be changed over time in profoundly harmful ways. For example, an *erasing of methyl-C tags* allows the oncogene to "turn on and take off." Once the oncogene is being copied and expressed, this change keeps the cell dividing when the same cell in healthy tissue is programmed to be phased out through a normally programmed cell-death of older cells, called *apoptosis*. Thus, the older cell, instead of dying at the proper time, takes off—through the nudge of the oncogene—into a fast-growing set of cancer cells.

Thus the oncogene switch is sometimes triggered by the loss of methyl tags on the oncogene. In other cells, *unwanted* methyl tags are *added* onto tumor-suppressor genes (which are designed to halt tumor-like changes), silencing them and keeping them from their health-maintaining task of curbing tumors.

To recap our discussion of the function of the epigenome, its central function is to control the expression of DNA, with its thousands of genes, in different cells. This role is connected to the eruption of cancers and other diseases, which we will discuss in later chapters, when we consider the epigenome in relation to human health.[3]

Another key dimension of the epigenome's function (one which is also a nagging mystery) is almost too astonishing to believe. It is related to the awe-inspiring process of growth and development of an individualized human zygote, which grows into a baby and matures into an adult. We now turn to this "mother of all epigenetic mysteries."

DISCUSSION QUESTIONS

1. The chemical formula of a methyl tag is virtually identical to what rather common molecule that is burned in the natural gas used in a backyard barbeque?

2. The discovery of "methyl tagging"—where tiny methyl molecules are added directly to some DNA letters—has come to be seen as a major turning point in the biology of epigenetics. Why does a methyl tag qualify as an epigenetic (above and beyond DNA) rather than a "genetic marker" (part of the DNA script itself)?

3. Why are methyl tags so important to a cell managing its own DNA, down at the level of individual genes? What role do they seem to play?

4. When the As, Ts, Cs, and Gs are being copied, as one strand of DNA is replicated into two strands during cell division, scientists have found that the methyl tags are copied over to the new DNA copy too. What amazing protein machine helps the cell accomplish this task?

5. Besides the acetyl molecules we met in the last chapter, we are becoming familiar with four other "chemical markers and tags" that are added to histone tails. Does the attachment and removal of these tags involve some complex cellular machinery?

6. Based on recent discoveries, what seems to be the likely relationship between methylation patterns and some kinds of cancer?

CHAPTER SEVEN

INFORMATION INSCRIBED EVERYWHERE

The Mysteries of the Zygote Code

Ever since scientists first spotted the new molecular continent of the epigenome and began landing on its shores, strolling its sunny beaches, and penetrating its dark and mysterious forests, there has been no end to the twists and turns, shocks and surprises. This fascinating voyage of discovery has been intimately connected with the question of how a stem cell—in our case, a fertilized human egg cell with its vast store of information encoded along the DNA molecule—can differentiate into all the types of tissue in a body.

For example, the human shoulder contains two trillion cells with various types of tissues—muscle fibers, nerve networks, and bone structures. Every element is brilliantly aligned and interconnected in a perfectly functional manner, with each tissue having its role to support and facilitate the normal movement of the joint. When we consider the shoulder's formation in the womb, and its ultimate goal of a mature adult form and function, we must realize that it all begins at the molecular level. Every cell must perform flawlessly to ensure the shoulder's normalcy, even though the very first cell of a human being (the zygote that comes from the merging of egg and sperm) has an entirely different set of tasks to complete, compared to the bone, nerve, muscle, or skin cells of a shoulder. What enables the necessary cell differentiation and placement to happen? What builds the complicated structural network that we find in an organ or an organic system? What sets up the unique life of each specialized cell within that system? Could the epigenome hold the answer to this conundrum?

The answer to the last question has become a resounding "Yes!" The epigenome has been shown to be the molecular key to the shoulder's development. In the developmental stages, each cell is directed to its unique use of the DNA files by the epigenetic system, which sits above the DNA but is in intimate contact with the genetic riches in the DNA. In a later chapter, we will explain how the formerly-called junk DNA plays a vital role as codirector of cellular development, working hand in hand with epigenetic information.

Furthermore, as scientists have made progress in pinning down the functions of the epigenome, another momentous truth has emerged. Even with all its complexity, its millions of tags, structures, and decorations, the epigenome has *more than one version for all the higher creatures.* In fact, humans carry within their bodies more than two hundred versions of the epigenome. This diversity was necessary because higher creatures have at least that many cell types. Cell types among mammals, for example, range from blood cells to skin cells, from bone cells to nerve cells. It is now clear that each cell type has a unique set of epigenetic software, whose instructions are tailored precisely for that cell. This fact may be the biggest shock to emerge from preliminary epigenetic studies.

The human body has an incredible variety of cell types—as many as 210 or more, according to some biologists. What this means is that each cell has the same basic genome, *but roughly 210 different versions of the epigenome,* each one modified and tailored for its unique cell type.

So, while the Human Genome Project had only one informational system to map (because the DNA sequence, with very few exceptions, is identical in all cells), a potential Human Epigenome Project would have a far more daunting task: mapping more than two hundred different informational systems. Though this seems an overwhelming challenge, a number of scientists have called for such a mapping project to begin at once. As a start toward this goal, the National Institutes of Health has allocated $190 million for a project called the Epigenome Roadmap, which is the first step in tackling the more massive project of tracing every tiny epigenome tag in every unique cell type in the human body.[1]

To recap the findings of recent studies, as scientists studied the relevant data and fleshed out the intricate production of complex proteins to form more than two hundred types of tissues, they concluded that this process—which differs from one tissue to the next—was not simply an "automatic system built into DNA." These processes that differ greatly from cell to cell are being directed from an outside source (outside the DNA) in order to effectively accomplish their tasks flawlessly—to create and maintain health in the entire human organism. This is the shock of shocks: that the DNA alone does not play the part of the director. It is, itself, directed by a system higher in authority. Now, take another deep breath as we move a bit closer to this "higher authority," and dig into its greatest mystery at the threshold of life.

REALITY CHECK: REVISITING THE OFFICE OF THE "CONSTRUCTION ENGINEER"

Though the term *epigenome* was virtually unknown to those outside the field of genetics at the start of the new millennium, by 2009 it had become mainstream enough to merit an article in the *New York Times*. In a fascinating article titled "From One Genome, Many Types of Cells, But How?" science writer Nicholas Wade notes, "One of the enduring mysteries of biology is that a variety of specialized cells collaborate in building a body, yet all have an identical genome."[2]

Wade compares the varied tasks of human cells to a situation in which different actors read from the same master script while additional instructions, above and beyond the script, effectively block the actors from seeing parts that do not pertain to them. Within a collection of living cells (analogous to the actors), individual cells do not need to see the entire set of genes (the entire DNA script, in this analogy). Thus, the portions of the DNA script that are not relevant to that particular cell—the genes that will never be activated in that cell—are made invisible; they are closed off by epigenetic markers. In order to develop the brain, liver, bones, heart, and many other structures, says Wade, scientists have concluded there must be a different set of hereditary instructions written above and beyond the DNA, which act to "open up" key lines of script in each cell, while making other lines functionally invisible.[3]

Wade focused his report on the DNA molecule, which we have compared to a massive filing cabinet under the authority of a construction engineer. In that cabinet are tens of thousands of master blueprint files (genes), from which duplicate copies can be made (RNAs), which are then sent to the machine shop, where skilled workers produce a myriad of tools and building parts (the proteins). Under the direction of the chief engineer, these molecules interact in intricate ways to produce every form of life. The mystery of how this molecular construction process is directed, and the selection of a specific master plan for each cell, has fascinated biologists for decades. How do the cells assign themselves to the different roles they will play throughout a person's lifetime?

In line with our exploration thus far, scientists have concluded that the DNA is not solely responsible for overseeing the grand operation, which involves hundreds of precisely timed steps to assemble the building blocks of life at the molecular level. A second system of information has been discovered—the very epigenome we've described. (Wade emphasizes the level of the epigenome embedded in the specialized histone proteins that package the DNA.) According to geneticists quoted in Wade's article, the epigenome controls access to the genes, allowing each cell type to activate its own special genes while blocking many of the rest. Scientists now believe the epigenome is involved not just in defining what genes are accessible in each type of cell, but also in directing the process of *activating* the accessible genes.[4] Using a familiar computer-age metaphor, the epigenome represents the software for the genome's hardware.

Thus the epigenome (the construction engineer in our analogy) directs the DNA to create the many different types of tissues in the body from one stem cell. If we switch metaphors to one of an orchestra, the director and musical score represent the epigenome, which controls the musicians and their instruments (the genome) to produce beautiful symphonic music. In a cell's symphony of life, the DNA files are activated and deployed on cue to build the cell's structures and maintain its health.

If each person has more than two hundred distinct versions of the epigenome, and thus has that many different orchestra directors deployed in different kinds of cells, each with a distinct musical score, this raises a question. How are the many different versions of the epigenome established in the first place? How are they rewritten after the initial epigenome begins its directing activities in the zygote? To put it simply, how do two hundred epigenetic directors unfurl from a single, fertilized egg cell? To pursue this question—the reprogramming of these epigenome systems—we must push back, further and further, into the earliest stages of embryonic development, starting from an original pattern laid down in the stem cell or zygote.

SOURCE OF THE EPIGENOME'S EXPERTISE: THE ZYGOTE CODE

Let's step back and review a crucial point, one that Nicholas Wade emphasizes in his *New York Times* article. We said the adult human body contains over two hundred distinct epigenetic libraries. Each cell type has its own tailored epigenome. Yet Wade gives only scattered hints as to what sort of brilliant, far-sighted software accomplished this feat.

What built-in molecular mastermind carries out this amazing wonder of rewriting and revising the original (stem cell) epigenome? Somehow, the original epigenome knows how to direct a beautiful stem cell into its rhythmic path of differentiation to produce dozens of different types of tissue in the body—but what system directs the rewriting of the epigenomic system itself?

This is a complex process that must happen dozens of times, as cells are differentiated from their starting point. Based on responses from the geneticists Wade interviewed, he says the DNA rewrites the epigenome when needed, and the epigenome in turn redirects the DNA usage in new ways as new cell types emerge.

Without completely rejecting this circular cause-and-effect pathway (we'll assume there's some truth to it), it seems an odd description of causality. What Wade fails to mention is the most important epigenetic programming of all. When it comes to the crucial, foundational role of producing the unique body plan of any higher species—whether a lily, a beetle, or a kangaroo—the key appears to lie in the *zygote and its interior architecture*. To be more specific, the zygote's three-dimensional structure seems supremely important. *Every molecule, every structure, every atomic nook and cranny of the zygote potentially contributes to the cell's destiny.* The precise molecular patterning of the interior of the zygote (in our case, the fertilized single-cell human embryo) has now been proposed by some biologists and embryologists as the supreme epigenetic code. It is, in one sense, the master code. Let's give it a name: the *zygote code*.

As we enter the exciting terrain of the informational mystery of the zygote, we are guided by Jonathan Wells, a scientist known for his pioneering work in this area. Wells is both a biologist and an intelligent-design theorist. He earned a doctorate in religious studies from Yale, concentrating his independent research on the history of the evolution controversy in the late 1800s at Princeton

Jonathan Wells

University. Years later, he completed a second doctorate—in cell and developmental biology, specializing in embryology—at the University of California at Berkeley.

Having published peer-reviewed research in embryology with his senior professor at Berkeley, Wells wrote several articles on Darwinism and the theory of intelligent design. In one key article, "Haeckel's Embryos and Evolution: Setting the Record Straight," which appeared in the May 1999 issue of *American Biology Teacher*, Wells underlined the importance of understanding (and correcting) the serious scientific problems left unrevealed in typical textbook presentations of the famous drawing of embryos by nineteenth-century embryologist Ernst Haeckel. Haeckel's drawings, though revealed as fraudulent in the late 1800s, were presented to unsuspecting biology students for more than one hundred years as key icons—persuasive visual proof—of evolution. In 2000, Wells expanded on this theme in his book *Icons of Evolution*, which reveals a pattern of prevalent misinformation in textbook discussions of evolution—with not just *one* but *ten* of Haeckel's so-called icons. In 2006, Wells produced another crucial work, *The Politically Incorrect Guide to Darwinism and Intelligent Design*, which serves as a helpful "crash course" on this controversial area of science. His third book on biological evidence that challenges the Darwinian paradigm is *The Myth of Junk DNA*, published in May 2011 by the Discovery Institute.

What interests us here, for the purposes of exploring the epigenome, is Wells's 2007 paper titled "Designing an Embryo."[5] In it, Wells summarizes the puzzle faced by biologists as they seek to explain the formation of an animal's unique three-dimensional body plan from nothing more than a one-dimensional, letter-by-letter DNA code. At the heart of his argument, Wells considers the claim that "DNA alone" can set up the developing structure of the new animal or plant that stems from the humble beginnings of a single cell. When the zygote is poised on the threshold of cell division and embryological development, there is a "structural goal in mind" within that cell—whether it be the stately shape of an elm tree, the sleek mass of a gigantic blue whale, or the fluffy form of a cocker spaniel. Yet, where in the cell are all these architectural plans embedded?

Wells provides an overview of the sparse evidence other scientists have set forth to suggest that DNA alone carries the plans for the spatial patterning of cells (which leads to the construction of a new member of a particular species). After reviewing the best "DNA-only" evidence, he shows why it falls short as an adequate explanation. He then describes several fascinating embryo experiments that point in another direction. A remarkable, non-DNA system of information seems to be at the heart of the cellular patterning-and-positioning process that precisely organizes cells, tissues, and organs. Certain structural patterns in the zygote (carrying what Wells calls "ontogenetic information") play a leading role in this developmental process. Especially important among these patterns is a key central structure in the cell called the *centrosome*. This spherical body, located adjacent to the nucleus of higher animal cells (including our own), plays a number of vital roles— one of which is to serve as the organizing center or foundation for the dozens of long beams, called *microtubules*, that give the cell a stable shape. Except during cell division, these microtubules are anchored to the spherical centrosome, spreading out from there in all directions.

To give us a clear and vivid picture of this debate in biology, we will return to the ISBiD laboratory to take one more super-miniaturized descent into an egg cell. On this trip, the guide is Dr. Ariana Lopez, a young embryologist who works as a staff researcher in Curt Grantham's lab. Accompanying her is Brad Seaquist, the winner of ISBiD's national teacher competition who missed the first voyage due to health limitations. He's now in top health, and has just reviewed a copy of Wells's paper, "Designing an Embryo," that had been emailed to him earlier.

As the two explorers suited up for the trip, Lopez offered a caveat: "This area of cellular biology is very controversial. Biologists who are committed to the notion of DNA as the zygote's exclusive repository of architectural building-plans tend to be resistant to new ideas that are outlined in Wells's paper."

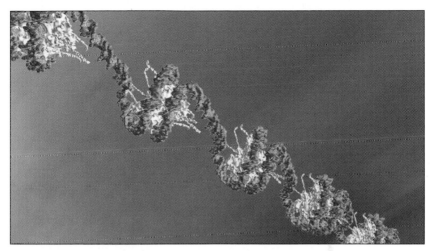

Figure A. Histones with DNA. Several histone spools are visible, each with about two full windings of DNA (in green). Jutting out from both sides of each histone spool is a set of four tails, which can then have code-like "tags" attached. Compare with figure K.

Figure B. Flagellum. A rotary-engine-powered outboard motor, built with forty genes, is in *E. coli* bacteria and other microbes. Biologist Michael Behe argued that this "irreducibly complex" machine points to design; it could not plausibly have been evolved, step by step, by Darwinian forces. Evolutionists then said a "Type Three Secretory System" injector pump could have been a precursor. Evidence has called this idea into question (see chapter five of *Darwin Strikes Back*).

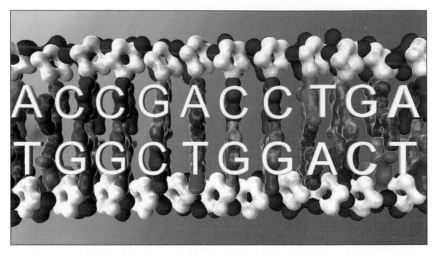

Figure C. DNA Chain. Represented here in color are the molecules that form a DNA chain. Along the sides of the ladder are the deoxyribose sugars (white) and phosphates (purple). The A, T, C, and G nucleic acids are visible in their symbolic colors: azure, tangerine, crimson, and green.

Figure D. Authors with models. Dr. Tom Woodward (left) and Dr. James Gills (right) pose with DNA and protein models. On the right is the tiny helical 21-rung DNA ladder, while the ten-foot model, a 75-rung gene, is pictured with its protein product, a 25 amino acid chain used in ribosomes of yeast.

Figure E. RNA passing through ribosome. The RNA chain is being read, three letters at a time, with the help of the transfer RNA (tRNA) molecules, having the shape of a "t." Attached to each is an amino acid—the irregularly shaped blobs at the bottom of the picture.

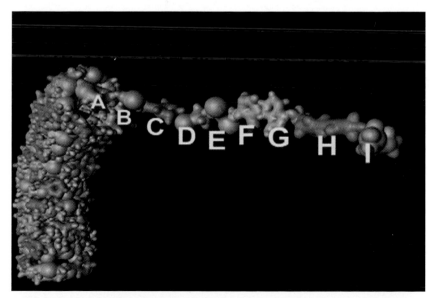

Figure F. Protein structure of flagellar hook. The protein that forms the "universal joint" or "hook region" of the flagellum is being artificially unraveled to show that the structure is formed by the bending and twisting upon itself of the protein chain. The "A – B – C ..." represents the different amino acids that are strung together in precise sequence, as if they were letters in a chemical alphabet.

Figure G. *Paris Japonica*. This plant was recently found to harbor the largest genome of all plants and animals—roughly 150 billion nucleotide pairs. That exceeds the DNA content of a human cell by nearly a factor of 50. © Martin Schneebeli. Used by permission.

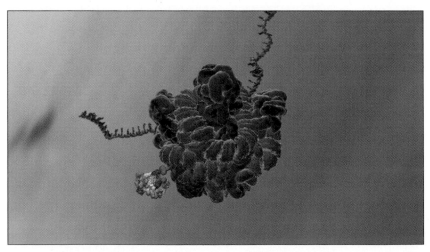

Figure H. Ribosome. Visible here are the *messenger RNA* (mRNA) threading through the *ribosome*—the "translation machine" that reads RNA copies to produce proteins—and the resulting *protein chain* that is exiting from the bottom and curling into its preprogrammed 3-D shape.

Figure I. Dr. David Berlinski. Trained at Princeton University as a philosopher, he has emerged as a polymath professor and writer who specializes in the history of mathematics and the scientific flaws in neo-Darwinism. As an intellectual agnostic, he has raised eyebrows with such provocative works as *The Deniable Darwin* and *The Devil's Delusion*.

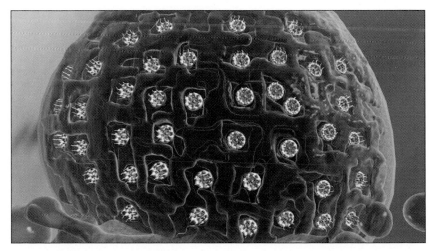

Figure J. Nucleus. This compartment for the cell's chromosomes is one of the largest structures in any eukaryotic cell. The nuclear pores, visible here, are like mechanized gateways, controlling the traffic in and out of the nucleus.

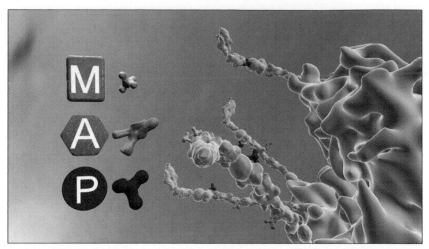

Figure K. Histone with tails and tags. This close-up of one side of a histone spool has had the greenish helix of DNA (see figure A) removed so that the tagging of the histone tails could be seen. Acetyl tags (A) are in aqua green; phosphate tags (P) are purple, and methyl tags (M) are magenta.

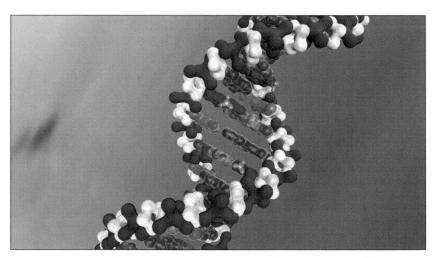

Figure L. Methylated DNA. Three tiny methyl tags can be seen on this stretch of DNA, attached to the crimson "C" letters. Methylation is generally associated with the "switching off" of genes in any given cell.

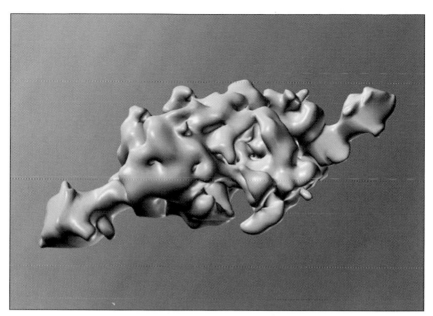

Figure M. SUMO protein tag. This oversized tag, which attaches occasionally to histone tails, is pictured with its characteristic goose shape. Compare with the closely related ubiquitin tag which appears in chapter 6 (see page 68).

Figure N. Kinesin. This protein, a motorized "nanorobot," is comprised of slightly more than three hundred amino acids. He is one of the cell's amazing workers involved in intracellular transport. Powered by ATP, he carries a huge load of building materials down the microtubule highway.

Figure O. Centrosome. This spherical structure, commonly located near the nucleus, is the anchoring center for microtubules that spread throughout the cell. The pair of turbine-shaped centrioles are visible inside the centrosome.

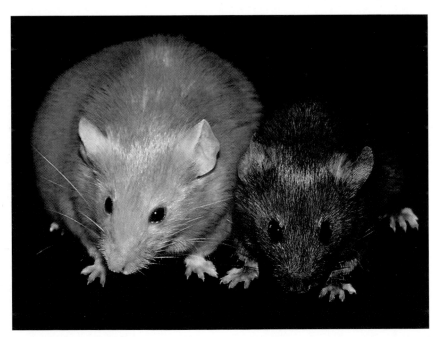

Figure P. Agouti mice. The obese mother mouse (*left*) had her yellow-coat-producing agouti gene switched on, due to a lowered methylation of the gene. Yet her brown offspring (*right*) had the gene switched back to normal function (properly methylated) by means of a mother's diet that was rich in methyl-donor foods.

Seaquist replied, "I can imagine! I just finished the Oxford Press book *Beyond the Gene*, which traced the storm of controversy that followed the weird research results that came out of microsurgery on a paramecium. I believe it was by a professor at Indiana University—I forget his name."

"You're talking about Tracy Sonneborn and you're right—his experiments on what he called 'cortical inheritance' caused a stir among many geneticists!" Lopez smiled as if she were savoring a private joke. "Maybe we'll have time to discuss his work during our descent to the target cell. Meanwhile, I think we'd better get strapped in our subs and prepare for the descent."

As the control room went through the pre-voyage checklist and Brad was safely sealed within his sub, he glanced over to Lopez's craft, and noticed that she was looking down at a piece of paper and grinning broadly. Curious, he switched on the wireless communicator and fired a question. "Dr. Lopez, what are you smiling about?"

She looked up. "I'm *really* excited about our special destination today," she replied. "I told you we were scheduled to explore a vertebrate zygote in the very process of fertilization—probably that of a frog. What I couldn't mention, because it wasn't confirmed yet, is that another kind of zygote might be substituted at the last minute." She flashed another smile and punched buttons on her instrument panel. "You can see on your master clock that we're less than a minute from launch. Once we're under way, I'll explain what's so special about this trip."

DISCUSSION QUESTIONS

1. Scientific analysis and comparison of the DNA in different cells is revealing that human bodies have just one genome, with a bit over three billion letters. Is the same true of the "epigenome" of a human body? Is it identical in different cell types?

2. Why does the attempt to obtain a "readout" of the human epigenome present a daunting task for those working in epigenetics?

3. Jonathan Wells and others suggest an intriguing view of the zygote: that the 3-D molecular structure of the zygote itself seems supremely crucial to inheritance. In this view, every molecule, every structure, every nook and cranny of the zygote potentially contributes to the destiny of the organism. How does this view differ from the dominant view in genetics today?

4. What are some of the experiences and achievements of Jonathan Wells as a key theorist in the biological side of intelligent design?

5. Some biologists have looked at the centrosome of a zygote as playing a role in inheritance. What is the shape and functional role of a centrosome?

CHAPTER EIGHT

THE ZYGOTE VOYAGE

A Sperm Delivers Its Gifts

In a matter of seconds, the launch chamber filled with water. Brad Seaquist experienced a mild feeling of queasiness and his ears rang with the eerie tone produced from the frame-shifting technology. With a muffled *thunk*, the two subs were released from the launch platform. Immediately, the autopilot system switched on, and the only sound that was heard was the quiet hum of the sub's propulsion system. As both subs gathered speed, a swishing sound mingled with the motor's hum. As Brad's sub followed Dr. Lopez's ever deeper into the gray ocean of the laboratory tank, he was still puzzling over why she showed such excitement about today's destination. He didn't have to wait long for an answer.

"Now that we're on our way," Lopez said through the radio, "I can tell you that our original target was a frog cell about to be fertilized. That would have been exciting, of course. However, by a special arrangement, we are working with an obstetrician who is assisting with a troubled fertilization of a single human egg cell. The only hope for success is to help unfold and deploy on the surface of the cell a set of key recognition proteins—the ZP3 proteins—that are not responding correctly to chemical signals.

"Once we've managed to help those proteins spring into action, we will descend into the egg to verify that the procedure worked. We may have the privilege of assisting—and also seeing up close—the launching of a living human being. In fact, we have a good probability of witnessing a whole series of spectacular events as the sperm arrives and the zygote is formed."

"No wonder you were smiling," Brad replied.

As the subs descended toward the egg cell, now looming large straight ahead, the explorers gazed at its smooth surface. The scene reminded Brad of a TV documentary he had watched on NASA space probes sent out to land on the planets and moons in our solar system. He felt as if his sub were one of those space probes and it seemed as if the living human egg were a small planet upon which he was preparing to land.

Within a minute, the living planet grew larger and larger until it filled Brad's field of vision. Lopez led the subs on a preprogrammed gentle sweep to the right. She took manual control of the navigation as she chose just the right spot to get ready to thread their way through the thick membrane—the famous "zona pellucida"—surrounding the egg. She explained that the ovum in some ways is rather more complex than ordinary human cells. As Brad's craft had reached the outer surface, he noticed that the "almost smooth" landscape was actually dotted with tiny tree-like shapes that popped out of the surface.

"I see lots of stalks with something like tree branches scattered here and there," said Brad. "Are they an important part of the cell's surface?"

"Very important," Dr. Lopez replied. "They are the rather amazing chemical actors I mentioned earlier—the ZP3 proteins—that act like super-sensors which help orchestrate the fertilization process. We will be giving several of these proteins a quick chemical nudge to help them unfurl fully. I'll tell you a bit more about this after we reach the interior. Meanwhile, stay close behind me while I do a little intervention here."

Both subs by now had descended all the way down to the very surface. Apart from the scattered protein trees, it reminded Brad of a barren desert. Up close, the surface texture resembled very thick tapioca pudding. Dr. Lopez repositioned herself slightly, so that she was in the middle of a grove of the treelike structures—they reminded him of weeping willows—huddled on the surface. As soon as she deployed a mechanical arm from the roof of her vehicle, the tip of the arm was unsheathed, revealing a small wheel. The wheel began to spin rapidly, scattering embedded chemical pellets in all directions like a lawn sprinkler. One by one, the calcium pellets triggered a chain reaction, and the sleeping willows began to unfold and unfurl their arms across the cell's surface.

"Terrific! Success!" Lopez shouted. "Now follow me inside as we move into our watch-and-wait position."

After the subs descended into the cell surface and passed successfully through the thick membrane, Dr. Lopez turned on her searchlight and encouraged Brad to do the same. She pointed out how the vast exterior of this living planet is held in place, like a vault of a cathedral, by means of long structural beams and girders—the *microtubules*. She explained that the unique pattern of these cellular structures is a vital part of the zygote code. Many dozens of microtubules seemed to radiate out in all directions from the heart of the cell, where the *centrosome* normally sits. She explained that there would be a brief pause in their trip, as she needed to take some pictures and gather chemical samples.

Taking advantage of the break, Brad piloted his sub closer to the nearest microtubule. He could see that it resembled a thick, round tree limb that somehow extended across the vast interior of an arena. Casting a glance sideward, toward the interior of the cell, he saw a virtual forest of these roundish tubes. As he wielded his camera to snap pictures of this array, he recalled something from the prelaunch briefing. "Wait," called out Brad, "aren't these microtubules the very structures that serve as the superhighway system of the cell?"

"Sure—you're looking at the cell's interstate system!" said Dr. Lopez. "Marching down these highways you may catch a glimpse of some ultra-tiny motorized proteins—robot workers, toiling at the molecular level. They actually scamper along these tubes pretty rapidly. With their help, loads of cargo are carried to their proper destinations. Perhaps you'll see one of these workers during our descent—be on the lookout!"

"I will," Brad promised, snapping a few more pictures.

Lopez said she had gathered enough data and was ready to move to the interior. "Before we get too far from the cell surface," she said, "I want to show you one of the surprising keys to cellular inheritance that Jonathan Wells and other embryologists have pointed out. Turn your sub by a half turn and look above you, where my light is focused. You are looking at the cell's *cortex*. The cortex has three parts: first is the cell membrane that we passed through, and second, the special proteins embedded in the membrane—remember the tree-like ZP3 structures we spotted. The third part is the associated fluid with dissolved nutrients and other chemicals. We call this fluid layer the *outer cytoplasm*. It's like a molecular sea that sloshes on the shores of the cell membrane and helps the cortex function smoothly. In a nutshell, the three-part cortex system is a foundational part of the zygote code. Patterns of vital information are embedded in the cortex, and we've learned from experiments that they can be passed on to daughter cells, even though the information is outside the cell's DNA. In fact, scientists have coined the phrase *cortical inheritance* to describe this phenomenon."

"So this isn't just speculation? There's hard evidence to back up this idea?"

"There is, and it goes as far back as the 1960s and 1970s, when experiments with very simple cells revealed this role of the cortex. You'll remember our quick discussion of the work of Tracy Sonneborn. The biological trick that he and his fellow scientists played on the paramecium cells was amazing. As the cells were near the time of reproduction, the researchers managed to reverse the mounting orientation of the motorized oars that stuck out by the hundreds from the exterior of these cells. You've seen pictures of these oars—the same motorized whiplike structures—called *cilia*—that line our windpipe. When the cilia were surgically removed and then replanted, they were reversed by 180 degrees on the cell surface. In other words, they faced the opposite direction. And yet, even though the DNA was completely unchanged in those cells, those reversed cilia in succeeding generations continued to face in the new direction!"

"So the cortex contains something like a blueprint that is inherited?"

"Your word—*blueprint*—is a good one. It even crops up in the scientific reports that were written up after the experiments. Two of the scientists who carried on this line of research after Sonneborn had retired referred to the cell as an 'architect' and said it 'not only makes use of the genomic information to produce the appropriate building blocks, but, in addition, also arranges the building blocks according to the blueprints as defined in the preexisting architecture.'[1] So it's fascinating that these researchers used the word *blueprints* to describe the layout instructions that were embedded within the cell's spatial 3-D architecture."

"And this information is not embedded in the DNA itself, right?"

"Precisely," Lopez confirmed. "Now that you've seen the cortex, it's time for us to pilot our subs down to the heart of the cell, following the microtubule on our right. This is our descent to the second level of the zygote code—to the spot where the centrosome itself is normally located. Stay close; you're in for a surprise!"

RICHARD FRANCIS AND *EPIGENETICS*: GOLDMINE OF INSIGHTS

Richard Francis.
Photo by Junenoire Mitchell. Used by permission.

Richard Francis, a freelance writer with a doctorate in neurobiology and behavior from Stony Brook University, has done us all a huge favor by burrowing into a mountain of technical, peer-reviewed articles on the emerging field of epigenetics for several years, and emerging with a highly readable account of this field. His book, *Epigenetics: The Ultimate Mystery of Inheritance,* was published in the summer of 2011, just a few months before our book's manuscript was finalized. We recommend it highly.

As we toured his goldmine of information, we found our own insights and understandings of epigenetics deepened especially in these points:

- "The Executive Cell." One of the most helpful descriptions, which resonated with what we had already written in several chapters, was Francis's picture of the entire cell—not just certain layers of the epigenome—functioning as an executive. We had sought to describe this picture already, but we found this description too important not to incorporate into this chapter.

- "Diet Factors." Francis deserves kudos for his careful research on the effects of diet in resetting the methylation patterns that sit atop human genomes. He analyzes, for example, the diverse effects on Dutch babies that were born to mothers whose pregnancies coincided with a period of near-starvation in Holland near the end of World War II.

- "Cancer's Complex Epigenetics." His chapter "Pray for the Devil" (which discusses the Tasmanian Devil and its facial cancer tumors) includes a careful review of the currently competing "genetics-focused" theories of cancer causation. Francis traces the potential complex linkages between epigenetic factors, and those competing explanations (the somatic mutation theory and the aneuploid theory).

In short, Francis's book is a ground-breaking masterpiece, which balances breadth of research with accessible prose that conveys complexities with the help of captivating science narrative.

Over a period of several minutes, Brad followed closely behind Dr. Lopez, trying to stay near to the microtubule without bumping into it. As they moved deeper into the heart of the ovum, Brad noticed that the other microtubules were growing closer and closer together, as if converging on a central hub or anchoring station.

Looking suddenly to the right, Brad spotted one of the famed worker machines that Lopez had mentioned earlier—the protein robot called *"kinesin"* (rhymes with "kind reason"; see color images, figure N). It was rapidly shuffling along one of the microtubules, headed toward the cell wall. Its body was slender, even stalk-like, but on its Y-shaped back was an enormous, roundish blimp packed with organic building materials. A tireless worker, the kinesin was managing dozens of rapid steps per second in its strange, limp-like walk. Brad saw that he depended on two floppy "feet" which managed the tightrope walk along the microtubule. (Dr. Lopez later explained that these feet are technically called "heads," but Brad agreed with her view that "feet" seemed a better name, given their walking function.) Both subs slowed their descent for a few moments to enjoy the spectacle and take some pictures.

"Glad you sighted him—but it's time to move on," said Lopez. *"Further down and further in,* to paraphrase C. S. Lewis! Now you can see that several hundred of the microtubules are delicately interlocking and interlacing in the heart of the cell. Over to one side, you can see a large sphere with hundreds of round portals on its surface."

"That's the nucleus, right?" wondered Brad.

"Yes," said Lopez. "It's one of the round bodies at the heart of almost every human cell. The other round body, much smaller by comparison, is the centrosome, the anchoring station for the microtubules. Inside its spherical body, two little barrel-shaped structures are placed at a 90 degree angle to each other, forming a "T" arrangement of sorts. We call these hidden barrels *centrioles*—they are a focus of research by Dr. Wells. He is convinced they are tiny turbines. Now, look carefully. Do you see a spherical centrosome in this part of the cell?" (See color images, figure O.)

Brad scanned the scene, looking for the place where the micro-tubules came together and anchored in a sphere, but instead, only a complex lattice-like conglomeration could be seen, something like a spiderweb. Brad saw nothing that looked like a spherical body besides the nucleus. After surveying the scene a second time, he ventured, "Am I missing something? I'm looking everywhere, but I don't see anything at all like the picture you showed us of the centrosome. Is it hidden on the other side of the nucleus?"

"No, it's not." Dr. Lopez smiled slyly and said, "I played a little trick on you—sorry. A human egg has a unique structure. It has plenty of microtubules, but according to recent research, it lacks a centrosome, which normally is the point of convergence for all those structures. So we have no ordinary anchoring platform for that network."

"Wait a minute," said Brad. "I thought the centrosome was *absolutely necessary* for the cell to divide and for a human zygote to grow into a fetus and then into a baby. So where does it come from?"

"You're right—it is necessary," Dr. Lopez said. "Cell division depends on it. So to become a zygote, either the egg has to develop a centrosome suddenly, or it has to receive one as a gift."

Brad paused, realizing what he had just heard. "One option is to receive one as a gift? From the sperm?"

"For the answer to that question, turn your sub around like mine and face outward toward the cell wall where we entered. I think you'll witness an incredible sight in the next few minutes."

Overhead, the cell wall looked like the distant ceiling of an indoor domed stadium, held up by the slender microtubules, but it was now developing a blister. As the blister spot enlarged, the surface changed both its texture and its shape. Soon it had developed into a huge bulge, which grew steadily larger, until—in a matter of seconds—the central cap of the bulge began to melt away. Where the cap was, a huge gaping hole appeared, like the crater in the center of a volcano.

Spilling through the hole first was the familiar form of a centrosome—an unmistakable smaller sphere with an array of stubby tubes jutting outward in every direction. It began to move down toward the center of the cell, looking like a beautiful star-like anemone or snow-flake drifting toward the ground. Immediately following the centro-some through the hole in the bulge was a somewhat larger sphere, with tiny, telltale pores; from Brad's vantage point, it seemed to be a nucleus. The zygote was now equipped with two marvelous gifts, courtesy of the sperm.

"Incredible! I think I'm seeing the capsule of DNA entering, with its twenty-three chromosomes," said Brad. "But it seems this isn't the only contribution. It looks like the egg has now received a centrosome, slipped in by the sperm."

Dr. Lopez confirmed this observation, and added, "Without this crucial gift of a centrosome—along with the sperm's half-genome, we would never see a true zygote formed. So DNA is crucial, but it's not the whole story. The centrosome carries a key part of the zygote code, and that part is very important. It helps prime the cell to grow into a human baby. I hate to cut short our tour, but we're slightly overdue for the return trip. When we get back, I'll share the highlights of a closely related idea that is emerging—one that seems radical at first. It's the theory that the 3-D positioning of every one of the millions of biologi-cal molecules in the zygote contribute, in one way or another, to the complete zygote code."

"I wonder," said Brad, "if this idea of the totality of the cell's 3-D chemical patterning, as the ultimate epigenome, may be related to the concept of the 'executive cell' that is set forth in Richard Francis's book you sent me last week—*Epigenetics: The Ultimate Mystery of Inheritance.*"

"Actually, that is one of many brilliant points made in that book," said Lopez. "In fact, I have Francis's quote in one of my new PowerPoint slides. If I recall it correctly, he says, 'In the traditional view, genes function as executives that direct the course of our development. In the alternative view, . . . the executive function resides at the cellular level and genes function more like cellular resources.'"[2]

"So it seems fairly clear, the 'executive cell' model articulated by

Francis and other scientists sits very well with our concept of the zygote code. Yet, in one sense Francis's concept goes beyond the zygote— it extends to every living cell on planet earth. If this idea proves its scientific merit through testing, and I'd wager that it will, then we will progressively uncover in the zygote and all other cells a global network of informational programming that boggles our minds—something that jumps to a whole new level."

DISCUSSION QUESTIONS

1. Why does it seem surprising or odd when we hear scientists suggest that the "cortex" (cell membrane) of a human egg cell actually contains vital information? What are the three parts of the cortex of such a cell?

2. One experiment that seemed to show clearly the inheritance of cortical changes—apart from DNA—was the surgical reversal of certain structures in the cortex. What were those structures, and what kind of change was inherited?

3. The molecule *kinesin*—equipped with its pair of floppy feet (technically called "heads")—performs what kind of task as it moves along the microtubule?

4. The surprise at the heart of the human ovum was that a certain key structure was missing, and was actually contributed by the sperm—along with its DNA. What was that structure?

5. In his book *Epigenetics: The Ultimate Mystery of Inheritance*, author Richard Francis has articulated a new view of the cell, which he calls the "executive cell"—where the cell at large is "in charge" of DNA expression. Is this idea similar to the idea of the zygote code? How does this idea go "beyond the zygote code"?

Chapter Nine

THE EPIGENOME AND HUMAN HEALTH

Cultivating a Spirit of Wellness

THROUGH OUR SECOND VOYAGE inside a human cell, we have begun to glimpse the multilevel complexity found in the epigenome's storehouse of information. We can see that the living cell possesses vast riches of life-enabling codes, which go far beyond the spiral thread of DNA itself. Information, in a diversity of usable forms, is lodged in virtually every corner of the cell, from the outer cortex to the centrosome, with its system of microtubules, to the histones with their decorated tails, to the methylation patterns attached to DNA. The mutual integration of these systems and layers of information is a marvel to behold. Unraveling these complex relationships will surely occupy the diligent study of biologists for decades to come.

As we exit this survey of the nuts and bolts of the epigenome, we have two more key areas to explore. First, we need to ask how the new epigenetic knowledge relates to our personal health, in both body and spirit. We will tackle the physical health questions in this chapter, and in the next chapter we'll focus on the spiritual and social health issues. Finally, in chapter 11, we will review a string of remarkable discoveries about DNA itself and the new picture that's coming into focus of a more sophisticated and complex genome than we ever imagined.

HERITABILITY AND HEALTH: CLUES FROM MICE AND MEN

Earlier, we profiled the emerging relationship between epigenetics and cancer. Since the 1990s, oncologists and geneticists have been focusing much of their research on this critical connection between the epigenome and the various causes and potential treatments of cancer. At least one drug has been produced that attacks the underlying epigenetic causes of a rare blood cancer—myelodysplastic syndrome or MDS—and it seems to be producing hopeful results.

In addition to the cancer linkage, undoubtedly the most fascinating and momentous discovery in the field of epigenetics is the heritability of epigenetic changes. In chapter 1, we introduced the work of Swedish geneticist Lars Bygren, who focused on family lineages in the sparsely populated agricultural region of Norrbotten in the extreme north of Sweden. His research revealed a link between patterns of binge-eating during bumper crop years and the introduction of a negative set of changes into the epigenetic systems of young boys during those same years. After correcting his data for certain socioeconomic factors, Bygren showed that in some cases thirty-two years had been trimmed from the average life expectancy of the children or grandchildren descended from the original group of overeaters whose heritable epigenetic changes were laid down as far back as the late 1800s.

Although there is still much to learn about such a tendency of succeeding generations to inherit changes engraved on their parents' and grandparents' epigenomes, a similar line of evidence has been found in studies of mice in the laboratory of geneticist Randy Jirtle at Duke University. These studies, which emphasized the importance of environmental factors in health and survival, focused on the epigenetic changes in expressing a section of DNA called the "agouti gene," which causes a yellow coat to appear in mice. Unfortunately, this gene can also be over-expressed, causing the mice to activate a biochemical cascade that results in obesity and diabetes. One of the triggers that caused the epigenetic marks (methyl tags) to be removed from these genes in certain cases was an exposure to high levels of a man-made chemical pollutant in the environment, bisphenol A (BPA), which is used in some plastics. In the case of some mice, this environmental "chemical factor" appeared to activate the epigenetic switch that led to similar kinds of unhealthy resetting of the epigenetic system that the binging behavior had caused in the children of the farmers in Sweden.

In 2007, an episode of *Nova* focused on Jirtle's lab research on the epigenetics of agouti mice. After the program aired, Dr. Jirtle responded to online questions from listeners, including many about the role of BPA in triggering obesity in humans. Two of these questions were to the point: "Does the [BPA] finding suggest that fetal or environmental exposure to plastics could play a direct role in a genetic propensity toward obesity in humans? Could there be a connection between the increase in plastics in our environment and rising obesity rates?"[1]

Jirtle replied cautiously that such a connection is possible, but has not been shown "unequivocally." Here is his complete reply: "We have recently demonstrated that exposure of pregnant mice to bisphenol A (BPA), a building block of polycarbonate plastics and epoxy resins used to make consumer items ranging from water bottles to dental sealants, significantly reduces DNA methylation in . . . mice.[2] This results in the birth of more yellow offspring, mice that become obese and have a higher incidence of diabetes and cancer as adults. Thus, there could be a connection between the increase in plastics in our environment and the rising incidence of obesity in humans. However, such an association will not be able to be demonstrated unequivocally until the expression and function of genes involved in human obesity are shown to be altered by BPA."

Fortunately, that was not the end of the research story on the epigenetics of obesity in mice. Jirtle managed to produce healthy young rats in the next generation, by changing the expression of their genes epigenetically—back to the normal, healthy setting.

What was his solution? In short, during gestation of the next generation of rats, he fed the mother rats foods that provided high levels of methyl groups—mainly B vitamins, including folic acid and vitamin B12. As we saw in previous chapters, these methyl groups normally act like molecular switches, blocking the expression of certain genes. Jirtle's lab results were startling. The methyl groups wound their way, bit by bit, through the mothers' own metabolic pathways, and were attached to the agouti genes of the developing embryos. "It was a little eerie and a little scary to see how something as subtle as a nutritional change in the pregnant mother rat could have such a dramatic impact on the gene expression of the baby," Jirtle said. "The results showed how important epigenetic changes could be. The tip of the iceberg is genomics. . . . The bottom of the iceberg is epigenetics."[3] (For a view of both the yellowish, obese mother mouse, and healthy brownish off-spring, see color images, figure P.)

This very question—the power to reverse inherited epigenetic changes—produced a fascinating exchange on the *Nova* webpage (see the sidebar, "Jirtle on Reversible Effects").

JIRTLE ON REVERSIBLE EFFECTS

From a questioner from San Francisco: "If environmental factors can influence the gene expression in offspring, can that process be reversed or altered by other factors (diet, drugs, gene therapy, etc.) after the offspring are born?"

Jirtle's answer: "We have shown that during early fetal development, maternal nutrient supplements of methyl-donating substances (folic acid, choline, vitamin B12, and betaine) or genistein, found in soy products, can counteract the reduction in DNA methylation caused by BPA. Nevertheless, we have not yet tested if exposure to these nutrient supplements can reverse the negative effects of BPA in adulthood."[4]

Jirtle cited evidence published by Ian Weaver and his research colleagues at McGill University, showing that there are other ways of modifying the epigenetic changes after birth.[5] For example, some studies have "shown recently that maternal nurturing behavior can stably alter the [epigenetic totality] in rat pups soon after birth."[6]

Jirtle adds, "Moreover, these epigenetic changes are reversible in adulthood following methionine supplementation or treatment with histone deacetylase (HDAC) inhibitors." (You'll recall we met the special HDAC protein enzymes during our up-close trip to histone tails in chapter 5.)

In summing up the flow of data, Jirtle says that mounting experimental evidence supports "the reversal of environmentally induced epigenetic changes via dietary supplementation or pharmaceutical therapy in adulthood."[7]

FOUR BASIC HEALTH GUIDELINES

Although the findings thus far are tentative, biologists have gained a solid, basic understanding of good habits and practices that promote epigenetic health. As we reviewed a wide range of studies, we noted that the published health-habit recommendations are not much different from familiar ways of achieving wellness generally. The difference is this: *caring for one's epigenetic health, especially during childhood, youth, and child-bearing years, can help to contribute to the epigenetic health—and thus the overall health—of generations to come.* With that in mind, let's review four basic guidelines for achieving a healthy epigenome.

1. *Smoking* has been shown by several studies to do extensive epigenetic damage. The negative effects of smoking are among the most thoroughly documented in all of the epigenetic research literature. This agrees strongly with what we have already learned in the past fifty years about the effects of smoking on our health.

2. A *sound diet*, especially a diet rich in methyl-donor foods (see, for example, table 9.1) is an important factor in maintaining a healthy epigenome. In fact, in genetics classes at the University of Utah, students are now taught specific ways in which their diet can enhance their own epigenetic health and that of future generations.

3. There is some evidence that a *positive mental attitude* can contribute to epigenetic health, especially as these attitudes reduce feelings of stress or enable one to handle stressful situations once they arise. Of course, this finding parallels a large body of evidence linking lower stress levels to general good health.

4. A substantial program (or a consistent life pattern) of *physical exercise* and maintenance of a proper level of body fat seems to be crucial for maintaining not only health in general, but also epigenetic health in particular.

Table 9.1. Methyl Donor Chemical Group and Food Sources	
Major Nutritional-Chemical or Vitamin Groups	**Representative Food Sources for Methyl Donors**
Choline Betaine Vitamin B6 Vitamin B9 (Folate, Folic Acid) Vitamin B12	Spinach Broccoli, Cauliflower Asparagus Beans, Peas Eggs (especially Yolks) Whole Milk Tuna, Cod, Alaska King Crab Chicken Whole Grains, Wheat Germ

NURTURING BEHAVIOR: A FACTOR IN STRESS?

The complex relationship between stress and epigenetics has become a hot new area of research, including a Canadian study of stress in rats. Moshe Szyf of McGill University in Montreal, working with collaborator Michael Meaney, has probed the relationships between rats and their offspring. Their study has focused on mother rats and the nature of their grooming and nurturing of their young.

Szyf and Meaney found that some mothers excelled at these behaviors, diligently grooming and nurturing their young; other mothers hardly attended to their young at all. Rats that had been groomed consistently as infants showed clear differences as adults. According to a report in *The Economist*, "Learning Without Learning," these well-groomed pups "grew up to be less fearful and better-adjusted adults than the offspring of the neglectful mothers." Underscoring a point made earlier, these changes were found to be inherited: "Crucially, these well-adjusted rats then gave their own babies the same type of care—in effect, transmitting the behavior from mother to daughter by inducing similar epigenetic changes."[8]

The second generation acted in similar nurturing ways toward their own offspring, producing the same epigenetic imprinting and epigenetically triggered behavior in the succeeding generation. Again, this shows that epigenetic changes, once initiated in a given generation, can be passed on to successive generations without changes in the genes themselves.[9]

The writer from *The Economist* concludes that Szyf and Meaney have made a "strong case that different epigenetic profiles resulting from early experience correlate with behavioral differences in adults," at least as it pertains to rats.[10] But what about humans? Can the same striking pattern—"nurture reshaping nature"—be seen in our lives? Szyf and Meaney believe such a link might be demonstrated, and they have begun studying the role of epigenetic imprinting in the brains of those who commit suicide, compared to those who die in accidents. They are also looking for evidence of epigenetic differences in the cells of people who suffer from depression, or who have violent tendencies. A link has not yet been demonstrated in humans, but if such evidence comes to light, it will have major implications for the mental health field.

More recently, another chapter on brain research was written when Richard Hunter, a postdoctoral researcher at Rockefeller University, found that "a single thirty-minute episode of acute stress causes a rapid chemical change in DNA packaging proteins called histones in the rat hippocampus which is a brain region known to be especially susceptible to the effects of stress in both rodents and humans."[11] Oddly enough, as Hunter studied the specific changes in one key histone tail, the changes produced by the intense stress were striking, but they moved in opposite directions. Looking along the microscopic histone tail, he found that in one pinpointed location, the methyl tagging doubled, while in a different spot along the same tail, methylation dropped by 50 percent. Hunter concluded that "the sheer size" of the epigenetic change suggests that it is key in the "brain's response to acute stress."[12]

"It's becoming increasingly evident, Hunter says, that the epigenetic changes like the methyl marks he observed and others, such as acetylation and phosphorylation, could play a significant role in the brain's response to stress and the treatment of stress related diseases, such as post-traumatic stress disorder."[13]

An equally revealing study of the link between stress and epigenetics was published by a group led by James Potash and Gary Wand of Johns Hopkins University School of Medicine. Their experiments, which are detailed in the September 2010 issue of *Endocrinology*, involved feeding mice a hormone known as a corticosterone in their drinking water. According to a report by *Johns Hopkins Medicine* writer Christen Brownlee, corticosterone is the "mouse version of cortisol, a hormone produced by the human body during stressful situations."[14] This hormone altered the expression of certain genes, which in turn produced noticeably higher levels of anxiety during behavioral tests. When scientists probed one particular gene—the Fkbp5 gene—they found that there were "substantially fewer methyl groups attached to this gene" compared to the control group of mice whose drinking water had no hormone added.[15] So, through changed methylation levels, alterations were set in motion that in turn affected a "molecular complex that interacts with the glucocorticoid receptor"—a key part of the normal functioning system of brain cells.[16]

The Johns Hopkins research group found that the epigenetic tagging of the Fkbp5 gene persisted for weeks after the mice were no longer receiving the hormone in their drinking water. This suggests the changes are long-lasting. According to Dr. Potash, director of the Johns Hopkins Mood Disorder Center, "This gets at the mechanism through which we think epigenetics is important. . . . If you think of the stress system as preparing you for fight or flight, you might imagine that these epigenetic changes might prepare you to fight harder or flee faster the next time you encounter something stressful."[17] Eventually, says Potash, doctors may have the technology and know-how to look in human blood samples to detect such precise epigenetic changes to DNA genes that are connected to brain function. As a result, medical personnel could predict or diagnose psychiatric illness, and perhaps target these epigenetic marks with drugs to treat depression and other mental illness.[18]

EPIGENETICS AND AGING

When we turn our attention to the epigenetics of the aging process, the evidence is overwhelming for a connection between the epigenome and human health. Researchers continue to analyze epigenetic changes that are tied to aging, but one thing is clearly known. Aging cells are characterized by an increased frequency of silencing in multiple locations of our DNA, through novel (and excess) methyl tagging. The effect is to silence genes that should be expressed. In other words, some cells in older individuals, due to the excessive placement of methyl tags on the coding regions of the DNA, have lost the ability to express a certain percentage of their previously active genes.

As scientists study the concept of the aging epigenome, it is clear that the accumulation of errantly methylated DNA increases according to age. Nevertheless, this pattern varies among healthy individuals and patients with certain diseases. Much work is being done to measure this methylation more precisely among older patients, in order to estimate the risk of developing various age-related (and methylation-related) diseases. These risk factors will be calculated by taking into consideration one's physiological age and one's exposure to diverse disease factors. There are significant hurdles to overcome before this analysis will be possible, but scientists continue to scrutinize the pattern of epigenetic tags and markers within the mature cell's crowded molecular ocean.

Another major goal for understanding age-related epigenetic patterns is the possibility of preventative options for diseases common to older adults. Can epigenetic reprogramming be achieved in adult cells? Can errantly placed methyl tags be removed? There is some evidence that certain kinds of drugs may be useful in altering the epigenetic processes involved in aging. As a result, it appears medical research may open the door to some age-related reprogramming of the epigenome. It is hoped that the clinical development of epigenetic therapy will eventually affect age-related diseases and afford some degree of longer life potential, particularly for individuals at risk for diseases known to have "epigenetic triggers."

As important as physical health is to each of us, it must be balanced with our emotional, social, and mental health. Ultimately, the array of health factors leads to the most important issue of all: the epigenome's relationship with our spiritual and social health. If this area turns out to be a powerful and dynamic factor in shaping all other areas of health, as we sense it might, then one could say we've reached the most crucial chapter of the book.

DISCUSSION QUESTIONS

1. Research on mice by Randy Jirtle has focused on the "agouti gene" and he's found that certain epigenetic changes have triggered the over-expression of this gene, leading to a "biochemical cascade" that produces obesity, diabetes, and cancer. How has he managed to reverse this condition in the next generation of the mice?

2. What are the four basic health guidelines for a robust epigenome?

3. Moshe Szyf and Michael Meaney have shown that when mother rats licked and groomed their pups extensively, the pups grew up to manifest an ability to handle stress better than pups who had received no licking. This has been linked to epigenetic effects of grooming within the gene-expression of the nervous system. What might this imply for human epigenetic health? Could there be a parallel?

4. Compare these two studies: (a) Richard Hunter's finding that a half hour of stress produced changes in the epigenetic signature on rats' histone tails, and (b) James Potash and Gary Wand's discovery that as mice consumed a stress hormone (corticolsterone) their Fkbp5 gene had its methylation signature changed, contributing to higher anxiety levels. How does the "stress linkage with epigenetics" differ in these two cases?

5. How does methylation (methyl tagging of DNA) relate to aging? Do genes become more or less methylated during the onset of old age? Is there discussion of medical intervention in the future to correct unhealthy trends in this area?

CHAPTER TEN

SPIRITUAL AND SOCIAL HEALTH

Is There a Connection with Epigenetics?

As we probe the connection between epigenetic research and the realm of spiritual and social health, we thought it would help to frame the issues by means of five key questions. The first question is preliminary, designed to clear a conceptual minefield. The others are more practical in nature, exploring the relationship between the epigenome and spiritual and social life-factors. We see these two sides as potentially influencing each other—in two directions. First, epigenetic discoveries can provide some of the most powerful evidence for the central role of intelligence in fashioning the biological world, which may lead to (or confirm) one's belief in a master creator of life. This new understanding of creation then may provide a key that opens the door to the dynamic relationships (and the timeless teachings on health) that are the essence of biblical faith.

Second, the cause-and-effect connection can go the other way. That is, we have studied the idea that a life of faith can produce attitudes and life habits that then open new paths to improve one's epigenetic health. A healthy epigenome then can be passed as a legacy to future generations. Sometimes these causal relationships can begin feeding back and forth, in a health-promoting cycle that gains momentum over time. This is an incredibly exciting area of epigenetics, but it's also quite controversial and calls for careful analysis.

QUESTION ONE: WHAT ABOUT THE "CG FACTOR"?

By the CG Factor, we refer to the "Creator-God factor"—a topic that's been touched on briefly thus far. We would be foolish not to address the case for a supreme creator of life—specifically, the evidence for a master designer of our epigenome. At the same time, by raising the issue of creation and religious faith as an issue of health, we know we're taking a step that is controversial. Yet, as we delve into the spiritual side of health, we know such a connection is not as outlandish as it seems. Many medical schools have begun to include elective courses on faith and spirituality as life factors that affect human health. The "faith and health" literature has expanded enormously in recent decades.

From these studies, a series of findings has suggested diverse links between faith and health. For example, according to research begun in the 1990s, certain kinds of religious (CG) belief produce generally positive attitudes and beneficial changes in life outcomes, including mental, moral, and physical health. This is especially true—measurably true using the tools of social science—when CG beliefs are acted upon and fleshed out in key faith behaviors. We are learning that when religious faith is not a static, theoretical concept, but rather is central to one's life and is thus developed carefully and allowed to flourish in all areas of life, it becomes measurable in its effects. We have been impressed, for example, with the research summaries on the many positive faith/health connections provided by Dr. Jeff Levin, professor at Baylor University and author of *God, Faith, and Health*. His work is so extensive and important, we have created a separate "God, Faith and Health" web page (at apologetics.org) to discuss the relevance of Levin's work to our own discussions on epigenetics and personal faith in a creator.

The connection between religious faith and human health, both at the level of the individual and that of society as a whole, has become a topic of intense debate recently. This is true both in pop culture and in the world of academic research. It is true that many atheist writers would seek to controvert what we're saying here. The group of authors known as the "new atheists" (including Richard Dawkins, Christopher Hitchens, Sam Harris, and Daniel Dennett) have charged that traditional theistic faiths do serious damage to personal and social health. Yet on this point, not all atheists are in agreement. On December 27, 2008, a provocative article appeared in the *Times* online, titled, "As an atheist, I truly believe Africa needs God." The author, Matthew Parris, a British journalist and "confirmed atheist," shared his observations from living in Africa and traveling extensively from country to country across the continent. After many up-close encounters in Africa (some of which he describes), he arrived at the following conviction: "Education and training alone will not do. In Africa, Christianity changes peoples' hearts. It brings a spiritual transformation. The rebirth is real. The change is good."[1] Parris's words on the "change of heart" are striking. To the extent that such moral, attitudinal, and spiritual transformation impacts health practices positively (and certainly such potential connections can be discerned), then we are seeing an atheist journalist acknowledging that biblical faith is producing changes that can contribute to robust personal health.

Can such changes be tracked scientifically? Surprisingly, moral, behavioral, and social health—as affected by faith commitments—have become a major research focus in the case of one key social group that is a heavy burden on society: federal prison inmates. Their behavior, which clearly has produced harmful outcomes for society and its overall health, is now shown to be measurably changed by a certain kind of personal faith experience. The study of the impact of a faith-based lifestyle on these inmates, as studied by Baylor professor Byron Johnson and others, has caused shock waves even within the academy.

ACADEMIC SHOCK WAVES

"Shock waves" is a fair description of the results of recent research on inmates who participated in a structured religious discipleship program in prison that enabled belief in a "Creator God" to become a central guiding and motivating force in life. Startling patterns of change have been measured by sociologists in what are called "quantitative criminology studies."

For example, over the past fifteen years, several important peer-reviewed articles by criminologist Byron Johnson and others have analyzed the tangible life changes measured among inmates who completed a spiritual formation program instituted by Prison Fellowship. Many of these studies followed the life patterns of inmates once released from prison, to see what changes in behavior can be tracked.

Several of Johnson's articles caught the attention of those interested in reversing the negative social trends related to incarceration and recidivism—that is, the tendency to relapse into criminal behavior. Recidivism is a massive problem in the United States and many other countries. When released inmates commit new offenses leading to reincarceration, it produces a cascade of costs to our society that goes beyond the financial dimension. The rate of recidivism was markedly and consistently lower among those who completed the Prison Fellowship study programs. In opening up this niche of research, Johnson has emerged as a leader of a new social science paradigm that studies the power of religious faith to positively affect negative cultural trends of all kinds. To date, Johnson has published more than sixty research papers exploring the role of religion in combating social problems, including "Religious Programs, Institutional Adjustment, and Recidivism Among Former Inmates in Prison Fellowship Programs," "Linking Religion to the Mental and Physical Health of Inmates: A Literature Review and Research Note," and "The Cumulative Advantage of Religiosity in Preventing Drug Use."[2]

These studies are remarkable in blending objective analysis with practical hope of social change. In the case of inmates who completed the Prison Fellowship program, there was a clear change: recidivism dropped from 41 percent to 14 percent. By living out a new life based on a love of God and service to God—and cultivating behavior patterns marked by love and service to others—these former inmates showed a measurable transformation of life that has sent true shock waves through the staid ranks of criminologists and sociologists worldwide.

These examples of beneficial changes to spiritual and physical health, due to the CG Factor, are only the tip of the iceberg. As we mentioned earlier, geneticist Francis Collins explained his own journey to the Christian faith, with its attendant positive life outcomes, in the opening chapters of *The Language of God*. (Admittedly this falls into the research category of "qualitative" versus "quantitative" evidence, but social scientists now are paying increased attention to such qualitative studies.) We have done our own qualitative study of the pathways leading to such CG belief among students and professors at Princeton University. In our studies, we especially noted and recorded the positive changes that flowed from CG belief and related faith behavior in the lives of a group of five Princeton professors. We focused on the area of spiritual health as it flows outward into positive change in the areas of intellectual vibrancy and curiosity, moral coherence, and social flourishing. The highlight of these investigations was a videotaped set of interviews that reflected the life path of each of five Princeton University professors who came to robust theistic belief. They have been published and can be viewed on the Internet.[3]

At the same time, much more needs to be done to research the life stories of those who went in the other direction. There is very little careful study of the life-changes, and the effects on personal and social health, that occurred among those who abandoned a formerly held belief in creation, and turned not only to evolutionary teaching (which can be theistic, of course) but also to agnosticism or atheism. We are currently conducting some research along these lines. Meanwhile, we recently encountered an extreme example of how abandoning a belief in a Creator God can produce a sudden change in life attitudes, which in turn affects one's social and physical health. We are referring to the story of Jesse Kilgore, a college student and vibrant practicing Christian, who was led in 2008 to reject his former belief in a creator after reading Richard Dawkins's *The God Delusion*. Jesse's biology teacher had encouraged him to consider Dawkins's perspective, which essentially can be summed up: Science assures us almost certainly that there is no God; theistic faith in general, and Christian faith in particular, are examples of a profound delusion, with no empirical basis whatsoever.

Shortly after finishing the book, and sharing with a few intimate friends about his total loss of faith, Jesse walked into the woods behind his house and took his own life. We wonder: if Jesse had been encouraged by his professor to read on both sides of this issue—if he had been given any books, articles, or DVDs that summarize the failure of Darwinian theory to account for even small improvements or additions in DNA or epigenetic coding, would he have entered this same spiral of depression? We believe that the likelihood of a suicide occurring in this alternative scenario is nil. We are persuaded that the vast scientific evidence—especially the genetic and epigenetic evidence—that points to an intelligent origin of life (suggesting the cogency of CG belief as per this book's argument) may prove to be highly relevant to future scenarios like that of Jesse Kilgore. That is, in similar personal situations, where "scientific evidence for Darwinian evolution" has been presented to a student as a knock-down argument against a creational or purposeful perspective on life, the epigenetic and genetic complexities of informational code, which suggest a code-writer, are highly relevant. You can read more about Jesse Kilgore in an article, "Jesse Kilgore's Story," on the apologetics.org website.

As we move further into the delicate territory of epigenetic evidence for a designer, it would be wise to make some preliminary comments. As authors, we have made no secret of our sympathies with intelligent design theory. We should note that design theory is somewhat different in content and approach from traditional creationism. How so? Scientists and philosophers who work in the field of design theory are attempting to analyze patterns in nature that are best explained as the product of intelligent design, and not an undirected natural process like the Darwinian mutation/selection mechanism. Yet design theory generally has a corollary (which is often not stated): as a scientific enterprise, ID theory declines to name specifically who the designer of life is.

This quasi-disclaimer may introduce a measure of confusion. Surely, a majority of design theorists are practicing Christians or Jews. Thus, when we say that design theory maintains silence as to the exact name or identity of the designer, this reticence does not reflect personal uncertainty among those Christian or Jewish theorists, nor does it imply a reluctance to discuss theological issues when the proper context arises. Rather, the restraint shown regarding the name of the designer is related to a diligent effort to keep science (in this case design theory) focused on scientific evidence. The sort of evidence that would identify Yahweh (or Christ) as creator falls into different categories of inquiry beyond the natural sciences; those kinds of evidence are analyzed with other methodologies. Thus, design theorists in general fully respect the power of other areas of evidence and other intellectual disciplines— scriptural exegesis, theology, and philosophy, to name a few—to shed light on who the designer is.

To make this point in a whimsical way, the DNA molecule does not have "Made by Yahweh" written into its text. The identity of the designer, according to our perspective as authors who are scientific researchers and also are Christians, is vindicated by reasons and lines of evidence provided by Judeo-Christian theology and scriptural data. Those data, for any who are interested, are presented and analyzed at apologetics.org (see the "From Design to the Designer" webpage).[4]

QUESTION TWO: DOES SCIENTIFIC EVIDENCE AS A WHOLE POINT TO A CREATOR?

When confronting the question of the origin of genetic information, one can view the possible answers as falling into one of two categories: (1) some sort of intelligent agency was surely involved (whether it be a creator within the cosmos or a transcendent creator beyond the cosmos), or (2) nature's design arose by undirected processes and the laws of nature—the interplay of matter, energy, time, and chance.

We have argued briefly in earlier chapters that the DNA molecule contains such a rich and massive storehouse of digital information that it can plausibly be understood to have arisen only from an intelligent cause. (We are using here a mode of scientific reasoning known as "inference-to-the-best-explanation," pioneered by Peter Lipton at Cambridge University and often discussed in the writings of Stephen Meyer.)

Quite a number of scientific factors and probability arguments point to design as by far the best explanation for DNA's specified complexity. They are well explained elsewhere, such as in Stephen Meyer's *Signature in the Cell*, or William Dembski's *The Design Revolution*, or even in Michael Behe's classic, *Darwin's Black Box*. In *The Edge of Evolution*, Michael Behe followed up his earlier arguments about cellular complexity and made a new and compelling argument about mutations, from new data derived from the study of malarial microbes, and the bodies of those humans who are tragically impacted by malaria. His argument is that random mutations are proficient at one, and only one, adaptive activity: *breaking molecular systems*, for temporary advantage in very special cases. At the same time, DNA-construction mutations, according to the studies of these nasty microbes who are at war with humanity, are completely nonexistent. The empirical data on this point are clear. Mutations accomplish absolutely nothing in constructing new genetic material or complex cellular equipment. Behe has not only discovered the "creative edge" of evolution, he has positively demonstrated the non-existence of Richard Dawkins's beloved "Blind Watchmaker." (For an enlightening insight into these issues, peruse Behe's responses to his many critics.)[5]

In our view, the above mentioned books by Meyer, Dembski, and Behe provide a devastating critique of Darwinian theory and an overwhelming case for the intelligent design of life. Meyer and Dembski point out that scientists only observe digital arrays of information arising from intelligent agents, not cobbled together by natural forces working through chance. The threshold for a single, minimally functioning bacterial cell is likely to be close to 1,000 genes, but it is certainly no less than 250 genes, amounting to well over a quarter million letters of DNA.

Can this quantity of genetic information be accounted for by mindless physical processes? Are the laws of physics and chemistry, plus time and chance, able to cogently explain the origin of the first cell? In the past two decades, the field of chemical evolution (which posits theories to explain the origin of the first cell) has entered a period of stalemate and deepening discouragement. This is the result of a simple trend. *The more we learn about the requirements for a single cell's informational load of specified complex sequences in DNA, the more a naturalistic explanation seems implausible.*

Noam Lahav, a leading researcher in this field, explains this scientific crisis in vivid wording that bears repeating. (In the context of his remarks, Lahav was clearly pointing out the need of a "new paradigm" to replace the current one that is in a state of disarray. As an atheist researcher, he has no religious motive for doubting the existence of a naturalistic or "no-creator-was-involved" explanation and was limited by his own philosophy for a nature-only paradigm.) Here is his moving summary at the end of a book-length treatment: "Having made a long and tortuous journey in search of the origin of life, some readers may feel disappointed: The alarming number of speculations, models, theories, and controversies regarding every aspect of the origin of life seem to indicate that this scientific discipline is almost in a hopeless situation."[6]

The sense that a solution is more distant than ever is common in the field of chemical evolution. So the biological design argument in general—and the origin of life problem in particular—is one way to infer the existence of a designer of life. If the same kind of evidence that points to a designed cell also points to a designed universe—as seen in the fine-tuned constants and quantities necessary for life to even exist—then the designer is not just a scientifically sophisticated group of ETs (as suggested by Richard Dawkins in the movie *Expelled*). Rather, the cosmic designer is beyond the universe; he transcends the universe because he designed and produced it from nothing. Furthermore, he crafted its laws of physics and chemistry. One should note here that, in a sense, even Francis Collins fully embraces intelligent design theory, in that he argues in *The Language of God* that the evidence of physics and cosmology points squarely to a universe produced by an intelligent, supernatural creator. So, in this sense, it can be said that the current director of the National Institutes of Health (Collins) is an intelligent design theorist.[7] Given the strong evidence for a creator from the universe's fine-tuned qualities, and even (we argue) from DNA itself, what does the epigenome add to this discussion?

QUESTION THREE: IS THERE SPECIFIC EPIGENETIC EVIDENCE FOR A CREATOR?

There are several ways that epigenetics connects with the question about the existence of a creator. First, one must consider the enormous explosion of the quantitative tally of information in a single cell, in light of the various levels of information encoded in the epigenome. If the single genetic code arrayed in each human cell is impressive, what about the proliferation of more than two hundred methylation codes, a different code for each cell type? Keep in mind that each methylation code in a human body has at least one hundred million, and up to two hundred million methyl tags, precisely placed on certain genes and other sections of DNA.

Second, one cannot learn about epigenetics without marveling at the exquisitely complex integration of the various levels of the epigenome in harmony with one another, working in communication and control relationships. This higher level of integrated complexity adds an additional dimension of apparent design to anyone who is not closed off to such a possibility by their personal worldview or metaphysical commitments.

Third, consider the relevance of the argument used by Michael Behe to infer design from the tightly integrated parts of *irreducibly complex* machines. To review Behe's idea, these cases of irreducible complexity are machines or systems that depend on all parts being in place and tightly coordinated with each other, and which could not function if even one part were missing. In chapter 2, we considered the flagellum, the wondrous rotary-engine-propelled outboard motor embedded in the walls of one end of an *E. coli* bacterium. This system requires forty protein parts, and each is necessary for total function. (So the flagellum grinds to a halt or is never built if one part is missing.) It is exceedingly implausible that chance could steadily form such a complex entity, adding part to part, step by step. Natural selection would never favor such a developmental pathway, since no rotary function at all—no locomotion whatsoever—is attained until all parts are present. (This example has become the focal point of a heated debate. See chapter 5 of *Darwin Strikes Back*, by Thomas Woodward, where this debate is discussed at length.)

Once we look carefully at the nuts and bolts of the epigenome, we realize that it overflows with examples of irreducible complexity (IC). For example, the IC argument for design applies well to the complex methylation systems that place, remove, and transfer methyl tags on the C-letters of DNA. To review the mechanics of this process, some extremely complex protein machines, known as methyltransferase enzymes, are necessary to keep the methyl code in place as the DNA is duplicated. When the methyl tag is found to be attached to a C-letter in a strand of DNA being duplicated, the machine moves across to the new strand, settles down on the corresponding new C-letter, and quickly attaches a methyl tag on that letter. In this way, the copying of the entire genome carries along both the genetic code (As, Ts, Cs, and Gs) and the methyl code (sometimes called the *methylome*).

How could the methylation system work at all if the necessary machines were not there and ready to go to work, so as to maintain the methyl code after a single DNA duplication? We are faced with a system that is staggeringly complex—irreducibly complex. The same could be said about a host of other molecular machines—many of which are very large and complex proteins—that add methyl tags to genes that don't have any, or that remove methyl tags from DNA. Examples of IC in epigenetics can be multiplied further: Consider the dozens of delicate operations on histone spools to carry out the addition or removal of acetyl tags, phosphate tags, and methyl tags on the various histone tails. A set of complex, exquisitely engineered machines are busy adding, deleting, or transferring those tags. Thus, discovering the epigenome is like landing on an entirely new continent filled with endless examples of irreducible complexity.

QUESTION FOUR: HOW DOES THE EVIDENCE AFFECT DARWINISM?

Another way that the epigenome provides strong new support for intelligent design, and thus collateral evidence for a transcendent Creator God who made us and cares for us, is the failure of the core of Darwinian theory to explain key biological phenomena. Although little attention has been paid in the media to this development, a number of biologists who are not affiliated in any way with ID have made it clear that they are looking for a new theory to explain macroevolution—the origin of new body plans. One such loosely knit group, which has collaborated to produce an important pair of books through MIT Press, has been profiled by journalist Susan Mazur. These scientists affirm common ancestry, but they claim that natural selection of random mutations cannot account for the rise of wholly new body plans and major organic structures. A wholly new mechanism must be found. Further, the epigenome adds tremendous pressure to the already-weak Darwinian explanatory apparatus. Random changes, inherited over generations, must not just explain the explosion of DNA as one moves up the purported tree of life; one must also now explain by these mindless mechanisms the rise of each sophisticated layer of the epigenome. If Darwin's theory seems to flunk at basic challenges of creativity, how can it meet these additional tests?

MAZUR ON DARWIN'S ECLIPSE

In 2009, the world witnessed a peak of public adulation for Charles Darwin on the bicentennial of his birth in 1809. Yet once the celebrations died away, it seemed clear the scientific discoveries about life's "horrendous complexity" had cast a shadow over the entire landscape of evolutionary theory. In some cases, scientific data have called into question the theory's very foundations. For example, a group of sixteen scientists who were profoundly dissatisfied with Darwinian orthodoxy met in Altenburg, Austria, in the summer of 2008 to find a new path of evolutionary understanding. None of these scholars are connected with intelligent design theory, but they have made no effort to hide their skepticism of the creative power of the mutation/selection mechanism.

This group, dubbed the "Altenberg 16" by science writer Susan Mazur, made it clear that Darwinism's highly touted mechanism has failed to explain the emergence of new organic structures and body plans. The radical views and goals of the Altenberg 16 meeting, and of the book affiliated with their efforts, were made clear in the prestigious journal *Nature*. Amazingly, said one scientist quoted in *Nature*, neo-Darwinism has told us nothing about the emergence of new body structures such as eyes and wings. Thus these semi-heretical scientists were laboring to move beyond neo-Darwinism—sometimes called the "modern synthesis"—to develop a new "postmodern theory" of evolution.[8]

QUESTION FIVE: DOES BELIEF IN A CREATOR MATTER TO HEALTH?

If there is indeed a creator of life and epigenetics, this makes a huge difference for the daily *flourishing* of human life. For many scientists, the knowledge of a new epigenetic dimension of the cell's complexity adds another dimension to the beauty of a creator's design. They don't believe that chance and natural selection can account for the amazing fact that the epigenome can take one stem cell and create all of the different types of tissue needed to form a human body and open the pathway for human life. With its sophisticated control functions that direct the use of different sections of DNA, the layers of our epigenome give the impression of an innate intelligence. So amazing is the epigenome that it integrates all the cells in a fashion that is productive, useful, and exquisitely precise in its multifunctionality.

The unfathomable orchestration of all these minute particles and cells combine together to create the beautiful symphony we call life. It's amazing to contemplate the extent of interconnected, multilevel design observed in the working of a single cell. We recall what Richard Dawkins said about biology in his book *The Blind Watchmaker*: "Biology is the study of complicated things that give the appearance of having been designed for a purpose."[9] Of course, Dawkins attempts to debunk the appearance of design. He is fervently committed to the notion that Charles Darwin discovered the key for explaining how nature itself, totally blind and unable to plan ahead, can mimic a watchmaker and produce the illusion of design. What's the key, according to the orthodox Darwinian theory?

In Dawkins's view, *natural selection* manages the trick, taking up the role of "creator-of-complexity." Yet natural selection has no long-term goal in mind. Dawkins admits it is "blind" (and because it is mindless, we could add "comatose"), and thus it has no purpose or foresight. It can only act on the modest digital changes presented to it in the form of point mutations in single letters of DNA. As of the writing of this book, there is still a thundering silence when one asks Darwinian biologists to provide experimental evidence that selection of random mutations can produce significant new quantities of specified DNA code. If selection cannot knit together even a few novel genes of DNA, why would we expect it to accomplish the feat of creating the entire genome or a multilevel epigenome?

We should note that when Dawkins wrote *The Blind Watchmaker* in 1986, he described the nuts and bolts of organismal and cellular complexity—the heart of biology's study—as prompting a clear, intuitive cry: "Design!" If cellular complexity seemed to point to design *before* the epigenome revolution, what about today? What shall we say *after* the revolution has begun, after that turning point is reached? When information systems are found to transcend DNA, but are beautifully integrated with DNA, what does this tell us? When such systems are detected throughout every part of the cell, does this not enlarge the impression of intelligent planning behind life?

Once the existence of a creator has been established, it opens up possibilities of supernatural sources of wisdom and strength, and it suggests that there may be a discoverable purpose in life. It takes the beauty of creation and human life that we have always sensed and makes them a door into a higher world, a higher life. In the movie *A Beautiful Mind*, Russell Crowe portrayed a mathematical genius at Princeton, Nobel Laureate John Nash, who was blessed with a "beautiful mind" but was tragically plagued with schizophrenia. By contrast, the mind we see revealed in the genome and epigenome is a "beautiful mind with no defects"—a mind that is the source of our own reasoning ability. Reconnecting with this mind in a nurturing relationship promises to impart well-grounded joy, robust intellectual health, and spiritual flourishing of every kind. In fact, the concept of a personal relationship with that beautiful-minded creator is an intriguing possibility that has been the focus of philosophers for more than two thousand years. It is a vital question of metaphysics that we will explore further in our final chapter.

DISCUSSION QUESTIONS

1. How can cause-effect relationships between the epigenome and spiritual or social health run in both directions? Might epigenetic research contribute to spiritual insights about the "CG Factor"? Do you think the life-impacts of faith might contribute to epigenetic health?

2. Examples were given of those whose lives or words showed the relationship between spiritual health and social health: Matthew Parris's article on Christians' positive changes in Africa; Francis Collins's story in *The Language of God*; inmates whose recidivism rate dropped after completing a discipleship program; and Princeton professors who related what their journey of faith meant to them. Which of these examples struck you as relevant? Why?

3. Scientists who work in design theory analyze patterns in nature that are best explained as the product of intelligent design, and not by an undirected natural process like Darwinian mutation/selection mechanisms. Yet design theory has a quiet corollary: as a scientific theory, ID declines to name the designer. Does this mean that design theorists, individually, do not accept the existence of a known designer (a Creator God)? Why do they not "name the creator" within the confines of their theoretical work?

4. What are some of the more powerful examples of "evidences of design" in the universe, in the systems discussed by Michael Behe, and in the epigenetic systems within cells? Does the epigenome seem to provide new examples of "irreducible complexity"?

5. What surprising thing did Richard Dawkins write about the realm of biology in his book *The Blind Watchmaker*, and how do those words seem to boomerang against the Darwinian narrative in our current understanding of the cell and of epigenetics?

CHAPTER ELEVEN

AN INFINITELY MORE COMPLEX GENOME

How Deep Does It Go?

OUR FOCUS SINCE CHAPTER 4 has been squarely on the epigenome and its relationship to human health. We kept probing the various layers and levels of epigenetic messages because that is the lead story we're reporting; it's our "headline news." Yet right below that story sits another huge headline, one that may be viewed as signaling equally momentous science news: "Human Genome Infinitely More Complex Than Expected."

In fact that exact headline was used on April 5, 2010, by science blogger David Coppedge on his popular Creation-Evolution Headlines science news website (http://crev.info). The occasion for this article was the appearance of major articles in prestigious science media a few days earlier. One of these pieces, penned by Erica Check Hayden, was titled "Human Genome at Ten: Life Is Complicated."[1] In the original context, the quote about genetic complexity being "infinitely more complex" than anticipated refers to the study of a single important protein, dubbed "p53." Yet the descriptive tag placed on the complex interactive networks of the p53 control system would apply equally well, we propose, to a string of new genomic findings.

Thus, while epigenetics has mushroomed in importance within

biology, the field of genetics has experienced a parallel explosion of newly discovered complexity. Just as our sense of the vastness of cellular information above DNA has grown, scientists have also witnessed an enormous expansion in their estimation of both content and sophistication of the genome. Here are some highlights, in quick succession.

RNA AS AIR-TRAFFIC CONTROLLERS, SCAFFOLDS, AND TEAM CAPTAINS

Some DNA reading (production of RNA copies of key stretches of DNA) produces what are called microRNAs. We have found that some of these have even been described as "air-traffic controllers," which guide the various other DNA gene products to their proper destinations, much as a traffic controller in a tower guides the air traffic around a busy airport.[2] Just as the once-ignored epigenome acts as an all-important engineer, directing the usage of DNA files, so also the supposedly unused stretches of DNA, including so-called junk DNA sequences, have unexpectedly powerful roles. They direct, control, and regulate the use of gene products throughout the cell's busy activities.

Meanwhile, scientists at Harvard University and the Broad Institute at MIT completed a different RNA milestone in August 2011, when they published in *Nature* a major study of hundreds of much longer RNAs, called "lincRNAs." These RNAs appear to play an organizing role in cell differentiation from the pluripotent stem cells, "acting as a scaffold to assemble a diverse group of proteins into functional units," according to John Rinn, an assistant professor at Harvard University and Medical School. He added that the "lincRNAs are like team captains, bringing together the right players to get a job done."[3]

A REVOLUTION IN THE IDEA OF A GENE

Genes are now considered more than simple strings of DNA letters. They are more like clusters of many diverse information modules, something like little microcodes, all grouped and precisely arranged in the same basic location, but with each microcode having potentially a completely different purpose than an adjacent microcode. Think of a page with twenty sentences, but each sentence can be used, ignored, rearranged, or reversed, depending on the higher purposes at hand. This "page picture" we've created is a crude sketch of how incredibly complicated our new idea of a gene can be.

Some scientists have proposed that we can no longer maintain the older view that genes are "discrete material objects." Their essence is not material at all; it is essentially immaterial—rooted in cybernetic ideas and information, and not in physical matter substrates. One scientist recently presented this provocative overview of the emerging picture of a gene: "DNA sequencing projects have revealed the gene to be a multilevel mediator of information that lacks a physical description."[4]

FILES, FOLDERS, AND OVERLAPPING MESSAGES?

Geneticists were a bit surprised to find that genes were arranged like the files and folders on a computer hard drive. That was eerie enough. But we were even more amazed to find that there are some genes (even in mammal species) that contain overlapping messages in the same string of DNA letters. Think of this as a string of English text—a long and complicated sentence—in a book you're reading. Imagine your surprise, when a friend tells you that the author is so clever that he created the sentence to carry two sets of information, depending on which letter you begin with. Wen-Yu Chung, one scientist who investigated this phenomenon writes in a peer-reviewed journal that the existence of these overlapping protein-coding frames is "virtually impossible by chance."[5]

THE EXPLOSION OF MICRORNAS

In previous chapters, we mentioned that what was formerly considered junk DNA has now been found to contain weird "RNA genes" that encode many kinds of helpful short RNA sequences that are essential to health, but which never become the templates for proteins. That is, their function in the life of a cell is not just to be a copy of a gene to be read by a ribosome; they actually function in the nucleus (or elsewhere in the cell) to provide key services—many of which are absolutely essential for survival. How many of these RNA files are there in a human genome? No one knows for sure, but one estimate is more than 450,000 such RNA genes are written on our chromosomes. The revolutionary nature of this finding is obvious. Gary Taubes contributed a key article in *Discover* magazine on microRNAs, entitled "The Sea Change That's Challenging Biology's Central Dogma." He makes this statement in the summary section:

> The implications are vast. Any disease that has a genetic component not yet identified—a long list that includes Alzheimer's, schizophrenia, bipolar disorder, obesity, heart disease, and diabetes—might be related, at least in part, by adjustments in genes that code for microRNA. Whenever researchers ask themselves whether microRNA might play a role in a particular disease or health problem, these days the answer is almost invariably yes, because microRNAs appear to be everywhere, part of the underlying health of organs and crucial to biochemical cascades we only thought we understood.[6]

THE SPLICING CODE

Next, we must note the way genes can be edited to produce different genes, or different segments of RNA, from either one gene, or from a number of genes scattered in other locations. This counts as one of the more important discoveries of recent DNA studies. For example, from one fruit fly gene it is possible to make as many as 38,000 different results—38,000 distinct protein products—depending on which sections of that gene are kept in, and which ones are snipped out. (The sections that are potentially useful are "exons" and the tiny spacing sections are called "introns." Scientists have been shocked in recent years to find information embedded even inside the intronic spacer segments.)

INFORMATION JOINED FROM
DIFFERENT PARTS OF A GENOME

In some cases of genomic research, we find that a portion of DNA from one location on a chromosome is linked to a snippet from an entirely different part of the genome (either elsewhere on the chromosome, or on an entirely different chromosome), to produce a final result. In some cases, different chromosomes bulge outward toward each other and almost seem to have an interactive conversation with each other, sharing segments of digital information so as to produce a new set of useful informational products. This level of integrated complexity is mind-boggling, and is further evidence of a very sophisticated level of information storage and manipulation.

WHAT? PSEUDOGENES ARE
FUNCTIONAL AFTER ALL?

Pseudogenes are seemingly damaged extra copies of perfectly good genes on an animal's or plant's genome. In some cases, a pseudogene has no healthy counterpart (an undamaged copy, that is) and thus seems to be an artifact of damage left through evolution. It would be something of an understatement to say that pseudogenes have been used as evidence for Darwinian evolution ever since their discovery in the twentieth century.

Thus it has come as a shock to find, in many studies since the 1990s, that pseudogenes have a function after all. (This undermines the use of the "pseudogene argument" for the truth of Darwinian evolution.) This trend reached a new level in 2010 when it was discovered that a pseudogene copy of a protein named "PTEN" acts as a helpful "friendly

decoy" in the functioning of the regular PTEN gene. This momentous development is nicely outlined in the sidebar article, "Brilliantly
Functioning Pseudogenes?"

BRILLIANTLY FUNCTIONING PSEUDOGENES?

A surprising function has been discovered for a "pseudogene"—an apparently mutated copy of a regular gene that till recently was thought
to be genetic junk. This pseudogene, according to a report in *Nature*,
not only has a function unrelated to the production of proteins, but a
function that could save your life. It is part of the tumor-suppression
system. Without this piece of "junk DNA," your chances of getting cancer go up dramatically.

The old paradigm about pseudogenes appears poised for demoli-
tion. The old story was that pseudogenes were relic "extra copies" of
good genes that, over time, started mutating away because natural
selection no longer acted on them. The new story is that at least some
pseudogenes are essential players in a complex interplay with coding
genes and other genetic regulators that control when, where, and how
much genes get expressed into proteins. *ScienceDaily* recounted the
old central dogma of genetics—DNA is the master controller of proteins—but said the new study "suggests there is much more to RNA
than meets the eye."

The particular pseudogene studied by Laura Poliseno and her colleagues is named PTENP1. It has a clever way of working to regulate
the coding gene PTEN, which is known to be a tumor suppressor. It
acts as a kind of "decoy." Since it differs from PTEN by a "mutation" at
the start of what would be its coding region, it does not get translated
into protein. It does, however, get transcribed into messenger RNA
(mRNA). As such, it closely resembles the regular PTEN transcript, like
a decoy duck resembles a real duck. The decoy lures the same micro-
RNAs (miRNAs) to latch onto it that latch onto PTEN. Whereas the

miRNAs suppress the action of PTEN, the decoys "un-suppress" the suppressors by stealing them away from the protein-producing gene. In short, "these findings attribute a novel biological role to expressed pseudogenes, as they can regulate coding gene expression, and reveal a non-coding function for mRNAs."

Isidore Rigoutsos commented on this discovery in the same issue of *Nature*. The commentary began by calling it "surprising news" that "pseudogenes are functional and could have a role in the control of cancer." While Rigoutsos noted that "pseudogenes have been presumed to be largely vestigial," he pointed to other recent findings that they are functionally connected to other RNA regulatory elements. Frank Furnari of University of California San Diego said this:

> Defining "junk DNA" is getting trickier. Pseudogenes, for instance, have been viewed as non-essential genomic elements and have mostly been ignored. Well, they shouldn't be anymore, according to Poliseno and colleagues, who show a clear functional relationship between the tumor-suppressor gene PTEN and its pseudogene PTENP1. This study could have major implications for understanding mechanisms of disease, and of cancer in particular.

Furnari also pointed to other possible diseases where breakdown of the tight regulation of the PTEN could be responsible. Two of those are human breast and colon cancers. He said it may be time for a "redefinition of this seemingly vestigial pseudogene as a tumor-suppressor gene." In closing, Furnari added, "The authors find similar associations between other well-known cancer-associated genes and their corresponding pseudogenes. They thus demonstrate that this unexpected mechanism of gene regulation could have broader implications in tumorigenesis and could potentially offer new targets for anticancer drugs."

Poliseno made no mention of evolution. Rigoutsos captioned a figure "Evolutionary relatives cooperate," but nowhere explained why PTEN and PTENP1 were related by evolution, how the pseudogene evolved a function, or how evolutionary theory enlightened the discussion or led to the discovery. *ScienceDaily's* article did not mention evolution, either, but instead depicted nature as a crafty designer: "The new findings suggest that nature has crafted a clever tale of espionage such that thousands upon thousands of mRNAs and noncoding RNAs, together with a mysterious group of genetic relics known as pseudogenes, take part in undercover reconnaissance of cellular microRNAs, resulting in a new category of genetic elements which, when mutated, can have consequences for cancer and human disease at large."

So is there another genetic code? This discovery multiplies the information content of the genome, because it amounts to finding another genetic code. Non-coding transcripts are now bearers of functional information independent of DNA. Maybe this should be considered the "third" genetic code.

The past decade has witnessed an explosion in observations of small RNAs in the nucleus. What are they there for? Since the function of pseudogenes, small RNAs, and regulating mRNAs does not depend on the parts that code for proteins, they cannot have gotten their genetic information from DNA via the central dogma. Pier Paolo Pandolfi of Beth Israel Deaconess Medical Center explained, "Not only have we discovered a new language for mRNA, but we have also translated the previously unknown language of up to 17,000 pseudogenes and at least 10,000 long non-coding RNAs. Consequently, we now know the function of an estimated 30,000 new entities, offering a novel dimension by which cellular and tumor biology can be regulated, and effectively doubling the size of the functional genome."[7]

THE RISE OF THE C-NOME?

Is there yet another layer of information inscribed inside the genome that we have not glimpsed until now? It appears so. In recent years, geneticists have begun to probe more deeply into the architectural arrangement of the genome itself. Instead of being heaped together like a random glob of spaghetti, the chromosomes seem to be arranged carefully and tightly in a higher-order 3-D specified arrangement. In a 2010 article titled "Genome Blossoms" in the *Scientist*, Cristina Luiggi writes, "Understanding how DNA is folded, wound up, and packaged inside nuclei provides an additional layer of biological information to what's written in the base pair sequences."[8]

Luiggi interviewed National Cancer Institute cell biologist Tom Misteli, who pointed out recent discoveries that come from a detailed 3-D model of a yeast genome: "It's a fundamental property of the genome to be organized, to be folded in some way inside the nucleus," Misteli says. "Now it's becoming clear that there is more to the genome than the sequence. We have to describe how the genome is organized, figure out the mechanisms involved in the organization, and then figure out how the organization contributes to function. Tools are being developed to really address these questions in a systematic fashion."[9]

Eric Werner of the University of Oxford concurs with this assessment of the new level of information in genome architecture. In a response to an article in a peer-reviewed open-access journal published by the Public Library of Science, Werner writes, "In the case of a building, the information for its construction and its structure lies not in the information that describes the parts that are used to construct it; rather it is in an architectural plan that is used by agents to construct the building. For humans . . . the information . . . resides in the genome, but not in the genes. Rather, it is in the network architecture that consists of coding and noncoding areas that determine the timing and spatial patterning of cells that ultimately results in the development of an organism."[10]

So another level of information has come into view within the genome itself: the architectural layout of the chromosomes and sections of chromosomes as they fit together in a grand, 3-D jigsaw puzzle.

CREATION: THERE IS MORE EVIDENCE THAN EVER

Each of these points of new genomic information, taken separately, constitutes a further compelling line of evidence for an intelligent designer of life, above and beyond the epigenetic evidence already presented. Taken together, the new DNA evidence suggests the image of an avalanche of data—the sort of evidence that seems to leap off the page, pointing us to a mind so brilliant and transcendent that it presses our imaginations to the extreme. Perhaps we are touching the edge of something so mysterious, so otherworldly, that our idea of awe itself is catapulted to a new level. Having concluded our grand tour of the genome and epigenome, it is time to take stock of what we've learned.

DISCUSSION QUESTIONS

1. What kinds of genetic actors (molecules) in the cell have been found acting as "air-traffic controllers, scaffolds, and team captains"?

2. What is the new "revolutionary" concept of a gene that is emerging? The gene according to this new view lacks a physical description but it surely exists as a functional entity. What does it do?

3. Besides the "files and folders" organizational system for genes, a shocking new finding in genetics is that *overlapping* DNA codes would be lurking in a mammalian genome. According to researcher Wen-Yu Chung, can this happen by chance? What does this imply?

4. How important are the new "microRNA" codes (and microRNA genes) in understanding genetics and treatment of diseases in current biological thinking? Evaluate the importance of one fruit fly gene producing 38,000 different protein products. Does that increase the potential information produced by the genome?

5. "Pseudogenes" have long been cited as evidence for the blind, random process of Darwinian evolution, since they were assumed to be "broken gene copies" with no function. What "shocking discovery" has been made about pseudogenes? How does this transform the discussion of this area?

6. What do we mean by the "C-nome" and why is this discovery so important and exciting?

CONCLUSION

Looking Deeper into the Known and Unknown

THE ERA OF THE EPIGENOME HAS ARRIVED. A vast new frontier lies before us. Scientists in many fields are working together to penetrate the epigenetic secrets—to understand the size, shape, and complex interconnectedness of this vast information system. At the same time, we have seen how the DNA storehouse is viewed with greater awe today than it was even five years ago, in the wake of discoveries of RNA genes, the splicing code, the functional nature of much "junk DNA," and especially the vision of the gene as a reality that is highly informational, but essentially nonphysical.

Now that we have brought our explorations of the genome and epigenome to a close, we shall take a series of final, penetrating looks into what we've learned. We need to look back briefly at the contours of our new knowledge. Then we will look ahead to the promise and prospect of future epigenetic breakthroughs based on recent evidence that has linked together two seemingly unrelated phenomena. Finally, we will take a look upward into the metaphysical implications of the mind responsible for all the wonders of life, including its rich storehouses of inscribed information.

A LOOK BACK . . . WHAT HAVE WE LEARNED?

We have explored the principal parts and systems of the genome—including its RNA and protein products, and even complex machines that involve the orchestration of many proteins into one system, like a ribosome or a rotary-engine flagellum. We then went outside the DNA, to probe other interwoven layers of cellular epigenetic information. We descended into life's ocean and viewed the five major sectors of the epigenome. Four of these parts concerned localized informational systems: methylated DNA, tagged histones, the centrosome with its associated microtubules, and cortex-based information. The fifth sector is really not localized; it concerns the spatial positioning of all molecules in the original cell known as the zygote. In this view of the "ultimate epigenome," different lines of evidence are now suggesting that *the 3-D spatial positioning of every biomolecule in a fertilized zygote cell contributes vital information to the offspring as it begins to grow toward its predetermined goal.*

We also studied how the genome and epigenome are linked to our health. Not only are aging and cancer linked to aspects of the epigenome, but many other diseases—and even mental health problems—are likely to be found tied to epigenetic changes. Such changes, in turn, can be triggered by a surprising diversity of causes, including stress, diet, chemical pollutants, and smoking. Ultimately, life habits and even mental attitudes of a breathtakingly wide variety may prove to be linked with epigenetic health, which in turn could possibly bear fruit—for good or ill—in the lives of several generations of our offspring. Though our survey emphasized the epigenome, we returned to profile major breakthroughs in the modern understanding of our genome. Chief among these are the splicing code, the role of the 3-D architecture of the chromosomes as a separate code, and the emergence of a new concept of a gene as basically informational—something inherently not physical, but nonmaterial.

A LOOK AHEAD ... WHAT'S COMING?

Many who have conducted research on the epigenome have confessed that, despite all the progress made since the 1990s, we still confront very large areas of ignorance in this field. Some have described our current knowledge of epigenetics as equivalent to the state of science's knowledge of DNA prior to the Watson and Crick breakthrough of 1953. If this picture is correct, we are barely entering the infancy of this field—a humbling thought indeed.

One largely unanswered question in epigenetics concerns the full extent of cross-linkage between different levels or sectors of the genome/epigenome system. Surely, many surprises await us in this area of research. One exciting, recently published discovery concerns the likelihood of a linkage between the epigenetic marking system of a cell and the splicing code. This possible connection was revealed in part by a study published in the February 2010 issue of *Genome Research*. Scientists reviewing a newly produced map that showed the placement of millions of methyl tags in a stem cell were able to identify previously unknown patterns of DNA methyl tagging. A report published by *ScienceDaily* revealed two very odd findings: "They identified cases in which DNA methylation appeared to enhance, rather than repress, the activity of the surrounding DNA, and *found evidence to suggest a role for DNA methylation in the regulation of mRNA splicing.*"[1]

The idea of methyl tags *promoting* a gene's activity seemed counter to much of what we've learned about methylation, and it shows how much we have yet to learn in this area. Apparently, there may be contextual situations (not fully understood as yet) that reverse the normal effect of the methyl tagging.

More fascinating yet is the newly suggested link between the methylation code and the splicing code. This reminds us again that we are still at the earliest, most elementary stages of tracing the links, controls, and feedback channels between the various cellular codes and levels of information. The role of methylation as a possible control system that helps to set up alternate RNA splicing was also borne out by studies published in late 2010, in which the same brain-cell DNA—found in both worker bees and queen bees—is radically changed by methylation, so that more than five hundred genes in those brain cells have differing methyl patterns.

Most significantly, the evidence points to the methylation as not simply silencing genes, but rather signaling to the cellular splicing system to cobble together, or re-edit, the pieces of genes differently, depending on whether the bee was a worker or a queen. The result was decisive: *the embedded epigenetic code orchestrated the splicing process on genes, so as to form fresh protein results, depending upon the brain's alternative needs.* Since the two kinds of bees—worker or queen—need to live according to different behavioral patterns, it seems that hundreds of gene products in brain cells are accordingly snipped and spliced along two different master plans, so as to prepare the brain cells for the two radically different ways of life in the bee hive.

With such oddities and cross-linkages just now coming to light, we need to be aware of how very limited our knowledge is of the genome/epigenome system. We can build on what we know, of course, but we should be prepared for science to encounter a long string of surprises as research continues to elucidate the interconnectedness of these systems.

A LOOK UP . . . WHAT'S THE ULTIMATE CONCERN?

Though the molecular ocean of life is filled with yet unknown quantities and qualities of complexity, consider what we do know about the incredible structure of every microscopic cell of the human body:

- An estimated sixty trillion cells make up a human body, and each one of these cells is unimaginably complex, and must live in community with its surrounding neighbor cells and tissues, flawlessly carrying out its own specialized part in the whole.

- Each cell is surrounded by a membrane thinner than a spider's web that must function smoothly, or the cell will die.
- Each cell generates its own electric field, which at times is stronger than the electric field near a high voltage power line.
- Each cell has its own internal clock, switching on and off in cycles from two to twenty-six hours, never varying.[2]

As we surface from our dive to the profound depths of the cell, with our focus on the genome and epigenome, we hope you will take with you a sense of the grandeur of the world that lies immersed in this sea of life.

Step back for a moment and gaze at the bigger picture. The mere fact that human intelligence, through scientific advances, is able to observe and decipher such intricate workings of the human cell raises another deep question. Where did that capacity for intellectual pursuit originate? Surely the likelihood is suggested that the human mind and its reasoning abilities constitute a glorious gift, granted so that we might know a greater mind from which ours is derived.

Steve Fuller, an influential professor of sociology at the University of Warwick, England, has spoken frequently (and published widely) on this essential "framing of the scientific quest." Fuller, who has no theological agenda to push and describes himself as a "secular humanist," has noted that the scientific revolution roared to life because of a central *theological* odyssey that motivated its founders. Fuller argues that Newton, Kepler, and other pioneers in science built their quest for knowledge on the notion of a universe that was created, and thus the study of creation provides the wondrous prospect of probing and approaching the creator's mind. Therefore, the driving force of the great revolution that launched modern science was primarily theological: *confident certainty of creation*.[3]

The fact that the universe in general—and the cell's micro-universe in particular—are constructed in such a mind-friendly way is certainly suggestive of a Grand Designer. The qualities of the cosmos that we are uncovering would further suggest that such a designer is not simply responsible for a universe that supports intelligent life; he also seems to have crafted a cosmos that is keyed to scientific investigation and discovery. He has constructed the universe, and the human mind, so that we can explore and understand the brilliant qualities that his creation displays. He enables us to discover clues of his designing excellence, his problem-solving brilliance, his engineering prowess.

The essence of all genuine philosophy begins with the human capacity to *wonder*. When one ponders the discoveries touched on in this book—rich layers of design upon design, from microscopic worlds to the macroscopic cosmos—one cannot help but turn philosophical and wonder. *What kinds of thoughts were present in the mind that designed all the building blocks of life?*

The depth of understanding of such a designer is beyond anything we can comprehend. We can only marvel at his ingenuity and inventiveness as we trace the seemingly endless integrated functions that are displayed across the panorama of the cosmos. Again, we wonder, *How deep does the design go? Where does it end?*

THIS MUCH WE KNOW

To draw the ultimate conclusion, we find that the only cogent explanation for both elm and elk is in design: an intelligent design, a design shrouded in mysterious beauty and yet predicated on a clear purpose. It is a wonder to us that our creator has given us such marvelous ways to discover him so that we can find him. In finding him, we discover meaning and purpose for all of life.

At that point, we also find the fullness of the intellectual quest and the life centered on truth, beauty, and goodness. When we view the material universe, and try to make sense of it, either as scientists or as non-scientists, of necessity we employ the higher moral and intellectual qualities with which we are endowed. The passion for an unfettered pursuit of knowledge, the respect for the unknown, and the humility of mind that understands how little we know—all three of these attitudes should characterize our continual search for truth.

In closing, we reaffirm that there is a unity of truth: scientific knowledge can be viewed as one side or "subsection" of this unified field of knowledge. Meanwhile, our knowledge of the master designer and his purposes fills a very crucial and foundational section of that same field of knowledge. Viewed from a Judeo-Christian vantage point, the division between the two is a simple qualitative distinction, and not an absolute dissection. It should not engender a polarizing or polemical spirit. Our mental grasp of the creation and our understanding of the creator (or, for some, the consideration of the *possibility* of a creator) need not be opposed. There is no necessity that ill will would arise on either side.

As Francis Collins has concluded, God must exist outside the natural world and the tools of science may spot clues of his reality, but those hints are not sufficient to lead us to embrace him in personal relationship. Collins noted that the ultimate sense of a "true knowledge" of God's existence must be based on an act of resting and confidence in the totality of his communication to us, not on mathematical proof. Yet, this path to knowledge of the creator can be filled with self-imposed barriers. For, as Collins writes, speaking of his own story, it was his willful blindness and arrogance that kept him from pursuing knowledge of his creator.

Wherever you find yourself along the spectrum of thought regarding the origin of life, we encourage you to consider the words of the apostle Paul, who declared, "Knowledge inflates with pride, but love builds up" (1 Corinthians 8:1 HCSB). Arrogance and hubris are never viewed as noble human traits, no matter which side of the argument they are. Paul concluded, along with many other biblical writers and millions throughout history, that an opposite trait is supremely noble and thus conquers: "Love never fails" (1 Corinthians 13:8 NIV).

God's love is the fountain from which our creation flowed in the first place. As we strayed and went our own way, turning our backs on his moral laws and principles, his love never failed. In fact, his aggressive, loyal love reached out to us. Though in ourselves we lacked any merit or moral attractiveness, God's love went so far as to provide an amazing redemption. (See apologetics.org for our own webpage, "The Creator's Love Lavished on Mankind," and link there to the interviews with Princeton University professors describing these truths.)[4] God's love purchased this redemption at his own cost and provided it to us at no charge. His purpose in all of this was grand and heroic: to complete, at his own expense, the wondrous, original purpose of creation. We are his "masterpieces of redemption"—we are changed by his own nurturing power, and our character is transformed as we behold the brilliance of his mind and the aggressive love of his heart. We need not toil, strive, or engage in endless hectic works to gain the creator's approval. All we need do is rest in his sure promises and enter a relationship with him. His "welcome home" is published far and wide. As a result, we may achieve the goal of his original creation, as we rest securely in his incredible redemption.

A FINAL CHALLENGE

Some who read these pages already believe in a creator; others will find themselves unconvinced of his existence for one reason or another. To emphasize the point made in an earlier chapter, the *first* library of informational molecules needed to form the simplest living cells would have originated by intelligence. This is an empirically grounded scientific inference, due to the "threshold problem" of a living cell depending upon no less than 250 or so genes—amounting perhaps to a quarter million nucleotide pairs. Have scientists ever observed the forces of nature knitting together wholly new digital arrays of information? Not once—not in empirical research, that is. Only intelligence can accomplish that programming feat—if we go by our real experience in all branches of science.

Conclusion

Complexity, irreducible complexity, magnificent complexity. That is what we continue to find as we penetrate the cell and its DNA, and then discover beyond DNA the methyl code, the histone code, the zygote code, and the 3-D code. This complexity only increases as we cast our glance wider and consider nature's unbounded variation and variety, such as the eye and the pancreas, human consciousness and imagination, soul and spirit. A mechanism of random emergence of traits, selected by environmental pressures, seems entirely inadequate to account for the biology, the chemistry, the wonder of it all. Darwin could not—and Darwin's intellectual descendants still cannot—explain the emergence of the twin phenomena of life and human reason and creativity. Only a prodigious intelligence would have the adequate, appropriate palette and paints to generate such a masterpiece.

Thus, a reasonable conclusion is that an intelligent being was the source of life. And if a wise, intentional creator is inferred from DNA alone, then all the more we would conclude that a designer is also responsible for the sophisticated control system that oversees the execution of DNA's information—the masterful, exquisite epigenome. To embrace the design hypothesis at this point is simply to follow the evidence where it seems to lead. The effect of this move in science is to liberate the study of nature from its crisis of contradiction, freeing it from restrictions that can no longer be justified.

As you close this book, we trust it will serve as a catalyst for a beginning of a fresh search for truth—new truth, deeper truth, rock-solid truth. After all, science is powerful in its own way, even pointing to a creator above and beyond us. Yet science falls silent when we ask such ultimate questions as

- What is the purpose for human life?
- What is the point of the universe?
- Why is there something rather than nothing?
- Why is humankind brilliantly equipped to pursue such questions—to analyze the conundrum of creation?

We encourage you to pray as you either begin this quest, or as you carry your voyage of discovery to a deeper level. Ask the designer to reveal himself to you—ask him to display his trove of truth and his marvelous purpose. Then, with an open mind and heart, embrace the beauty of that truth and purpose that you find. The deeper you look, the more the glow of God's presence will color your world and light your way.

DISCUSSION QUESTIONS

1. Four parts of the epigenome are specific levels, and one is more diffuse, across the entire space of a zygote. What are these four specific levels? What is the nature of the fifth level of information?

2. Some have compared our current knowledge of the epigenome with the state of knowledge of DNA before Watson and Crick discovered the molecule's double helix structure. Assuming that this is so, discuss why this is so humbling, and what this hints about the future of epigenetic research.

3. Recent findings suggest that methylation patterns are presenting some odd findings in the way they act differently in different contexts, and can even help regulate another code. What is the other code that methylation seems to help control, and what does this tell us about the integrated complexity of the "overall design" of the cell?

4. According to Steve Fuller, was the idea of a "created universe" a healthy concept for science, helping the scientific revolution to take off, or was it a detriment? Discuss why and how this is so.

5. Discuss what the relationship should look like between the two fields of knowledge discussed here: a mental grasp of the creation, and a knowledge of the creator. According to Francis Collins, what is a "true knowledge" of God based on, and what was the personal barrier he struggled with in considering this?

6. What are the spiritual implications of pondering and wondering about the magnificent complexity of life? What new vistas are opened to us?

APPENDIX

Some Frequently Asked Questions

Some scholars have focused on the role of epigenetics in producing the changes in health and physiology of identical (monozygotic) twins. The pattern of increasing differences between such twins during their lifetimes has been linked to changes in methylation patterns of DNA. Is there good evidence for this?

Yes, a growing body of evidence is showing how changes are brought about in the epigenomes of identical twins that may trigger modifications in physiology, such as differences in fertility and time of menopause for women, or in the appearance of diseases such as schizophrenia, cancer, or bipolar disorder. A team of researchers in Spain, led by Dr. Manel Esteller, conducted epigenetic studies on forty pairs of identical twins who were at different stages of life. Their study, published in July 2005, showed clear patterns of differing methylation of twins' DNA, and the differences increased with age. So epigenetic changes are indicated as one key factor in the divergence of the health history of identical twins during their lifetimes.

Appendix

Some evolutionary theorists see "epigenetic inheritance" as giving new life to the old idea of Lamarckian evolution—the inheritance of acquired traits. What valid parallels are there between these two concepts?

There are superficial parallels between the two. In 1809 French zoologist Jean-Baptiste Lamarck proposed a theory of evolution by the inheritance of characteristics that were acquired by one generation and then passed on to the next generation. Darwin himself left the door open for Lamarckian evolution (he used the term *pangenesis*) to play a minor role in evolutionary change. By the time the neo-Darwinian Synthesis developed in the 1940s, Lamarckian evolution was viewed as a quaint but completely discredited idea. With the emergence of the epigenetics revolution, however, some biologists see epigenetic inheritance playing a key role in evolution, one that has an eerie similarity to Lamarck's ideas. Science historian Eva Jablonka has traced these ideas in her important book *Evolution in Four Dimensions*.

So . . . what do you make of epigenetics as a potential "Lamarckian-type" evolutionary mechanism? Can epigenetic changes contribute to evolutionary novelty?

It all depends on what one means by the weasel word "evolution." If one simply means "change over time" or "minor modifications [such as size, shape] of existing organs," then surely epigenetic switches can cause such modest changes. Yet the word usually means something far more expansive: *unguided macroevolution of all living things from a common ancestor*—starting with the single-celled "LUCA" (Last Universal Common Ancestor). At this level, it seems quite implausible that changes in the patterns of epigenetic switches could play any role in writing the specified code in DNA to produce the thousands of novel genes needed for the precise proteins upon which all variation in biology depends. To sum up, epigenetics may affect "the survival of the fittest," but it cannot explain "the arrival of the fittest."

Some Frequently Asked Questions

What are the most authoritative books in print which address the topic of epigenetics from an advanced level?

Our research was aided by several scholarly books: *The Epigenome: Molecular Hide and Seek,* edited by Stephan Beck and Alexander Olek, (Wiley-VCH, 2003); *Epigenetics,* edited by C. David Allis, Thomas Jenuwein, and Danny Reinberg (Cold Spring Harbor Laboratory Press, 2007); and, more recently, the *Handbook of Epigenetics,* edited by Trygve Tollefsbol, with thirty-seven collected articles (Academic Press, 2010). All of these are written for those having a strong biological education. An outstanding introduction is found in Richard Francis's *Epigenetics: The Ultimate Mystery of Inheritance* (W. W. Norton & Co., 2011).

What actually guides the changes that are made to the epigenetic markings in DNA and chromatin, as cell differentiation takes place? Do scientists fully understand this process?

To answer the second question, no, scientists do not yet fully grasp this dynamic process. Yet we have learned much in the past decade. This is the central focus of much epigenetic research, and the process that is coming into view seems to be extraordinarily complex, involving networks of regulatory genes (with their protein products) integrated with the toiling of a wide variety of RNA molecules, so that the various tag-placing proteins know exactly where and when to place their epigenetic tags during cell differentiation. To answer this question in more detail would require an additional chapter, if not another entire book.

NOTES

INTRODUCTION: BEYOND DNA

1. "The Decision to Go to the Moon: President John F. Kennedy's May 25, 1961 Speech before a Joint Session of Congress," National Aeronautics and Space Administration (NASA) History Office, history.nasa.gov /moondec.html.

2. Nicholas Wade, "A Decade Later, Genetic Map Yields Few New Cures," *New York Times*, June 12, 2010, http://www.nytimes.com/2010/06/13/ health/research/13genome.html.

CHAPTER ONE: SCIENCE'S SUPREME QUEST

1. John Cloud, "Why Your DNA Isn't Your Destiny," *Time*, January 6, 2010, http://www.time.com/time/health/article/0,8599,1951968,00.html.

2. "New Findings Challenge Established Views on Human Genome: EN-CODE Research Consortium Uncovers Surprises Related to Organization and Function of Human Genetic Blueprint," NIH News Release, June 13, 2007, http://genome.gov/25521554 (accessed August 1, 2011).

3. For example, in *The Language of God*, by evangelical Christian and former Human Genome Project director Francis Collins, the intelligent design theory is described as a ship that is not "headed to the promised land" but is headed "to the bottom of the sea." We will have occasion to return to Dr. Collins's vigorous defense of Darwinism a bit later, and we will point out serious scientific problems with this chapter, but it is enough here to note that he is merely the most visible (and well known)

member of a movement of scientists and Christian leaders, many of them associated with the BioLogos website, who call on Christians to cease their questioning of the scientific claims of Darwinian evolution. We view this development as educationally and empirically astonishing, in light of the crucial void of evidence for a vast creative power of the mutation-selection mechanism. Leaving theological questions aside, why should Christian theists make peace with a theory that is scientifically in tatters?

4. See the articles, from crev.info news blog, archived at apologetics.org. Click on the home page link to "Beyond the Genome: Key Resources."

5. Michael Behe, *Darwin's Black Box* (New York: Free Press, 2006), 24.

CHAPTER TWO: WHAT BIOLOGISTS KNOW ABOUT DNA

1. The idea of a scientist who is an atheist coming to the defense of intelligent design is not imaginary. The comments from the imaginary physicist here are based on an actual occurrence. In early 2010, on the weekly Darwin or Design radio program, Dr. Woodward interviewed Dr. Bradley Monton, professor of the philosophy of physics at the University of Colorado (Boulder). Dr. Monton earned his doctorate in that field at Princeton University and has become renowned as a secular defender of the scientific legitimacy of design theory. His book, *Seeking God in Science: An Atheist Defends Intelligent Design* presents a balanced and sober evaluation of a wide array of ID arguments—both in biology and physics. Monton believes that a number of these arguments, especially the ones in physics and cosmology, carry some weight and could prove to be right in the long run, though he personally is not yet convinced to abandon his atheism.

2. For a picture of two hand-held models of DNA we've developed, a shorter one with twenty-one rungs, and a longer, ten-foot model of a pygmy gene with seventy-five rungs (side by side with a model of the protein it produces), see figure D.

3. Construction directions entitled "How to Build a Sweet DNA Model" can be found on the apologetics.org website.

4. Michael Behe, *Darwin's Black Box* (New York: Free Press, 2006), 255.

CHAPTER THREE: TWO GRAND, UNSUNG HEROES

1. Richard Francis, *Epigenetics* (New York: W. W. Norton, 2011), 21.
2. Another barrel-shaped machine, a chaperone protein, often jumps into the action and works like a mechanized "dressing room," helping the protein fold in its private compartment.

CHAPTER FOUR: A VAST INFORMATIONAL ICEBERG

1. Dawkins and his fellow atheologians say that parents who take their children to church or instruct them in religion are engaging in a form of child abuse. These ferocious attitudes seemed to explode from a recent string of books, produced by Dawkins and his fellow "new atheists": Sam Harris, Christopher Hitchens, and Daniel Dennett.
2. This set of quotes is found in many published and electronic articles and book chapters. See, for example, the opening paragraphs of Jonathan Wells's "Darwin of the Gaps," http:///www.discovery.org/a/4529 (accessed August 1, 2011).
3. See John West, "What Are the Religious Views of Leading Scientists Who Support Evolution?" Discovery Institute, May 1, 2009, www .discovery.org/a/10171 (accessed August 31, 2011). John West points out in his article that outside the elite circle of NAS biologists, the rate of atheism drops somewhat, but it still remains much higher than what is found in the general US population. For example, the results of a Cornell Evolution Project Survey, one of several discussed in West's report, show that 87 percent of those polled, all of whom were described as leading biologists in the field of evolution, deny the existence of God.
4. See James P. Gills and Thomas Woodward, *Darwinism Under the Microscope* (2002). See also Gills, *Exceeding Gratitude for the Creator's Plan* (2007), and Woodward, *Doubts About Darwin* (2003) and *Darwin Strikes Back* (2006).
5. See Thomas Woodward, *Darwin Strikes Back: Defending the Science of Intelligent Design* (Grand Rapids: Baker, 2006), chapters 3 and 4.

6. See Douglas D. Axe, "Extreme Functional Sensitivity to Conservative Amino Acid Changes on Enzyme Exteriors," *Journal of Molecular Biology* 301 (2000): 585–95; Douglas D. Axe, "Estimating the Prevalence of Protein Sequences Adopting Functional Enzyme Folds," *Journal of Molecular Biology* 341 (2004): 1295–315. Perhaps the most important work published in this area is an article by Douglas D. Axe, "The Case Against a Darwinian Origin of Protein Folds," *Bio-Complexity* 2010, no. 1 (April 15, 2010), http://bio-complexity.org/ojs/index.php/main /article/view/BIO-C.2010.1.

7. One such limitation refers to the dominant geological version of uniformitarianism, which seemed to reject, a priori, the possibility of catastrophic (local or global) processes in the history of life. Virtually all of science depends, at least as a faith construct, on the uniformitarian aspect of the laws of nature remaining constant in time and space. However, geological uniformitarianism has come under fire in the past century, and most geologists have become much more open to the idea of repeated local catastrophic events playing a part in geological formation.

8. See "Genome Sizes" at http://users.rcn.com/jkimball.ma.ultranet/Bio logyPages/G/GenomeSizes.html (last updated February 3, 2011) by John W. Kimball, author of *Biology*, 6th ed. (Dubuque, IA: Wm. C. Brown, 1994).

9. John Cloud, "Why Your DNA Isn't Your Destiny," *Time*, January 6, 2010, http://www.time.com/time/health/article/0,8599,1951968,00.html.

CHAPTER SIX: THE FIFTH LETTER OF DNA

1. "Epigenetic Therapy," NOVA Online, posted October 16, 2007, www .pbs.org/wgbh/nova/genes/issa.html. The interview with Dr. Jean-Pierre Issa was conducted on January 8, 2007, by Sarah Holt, and edited by Lauren Aguirre.

2. For a helpful introductory overview of oncogenes and tumor suppressor genes, see "Oncogenes, Turmor Suppressor Genes, and Cancer," American Cancer Society, July 8, 2009, http://www.cancer.org/acs/groups /cid/documents/webcontent/002550-pdf.pdf

3. For an overview of the role of the epigenome in the development and control of cancer, see Peter A. Jones and Stephen B. Baylin, "The Epigenomics of Cancer," *Cell* 128, no. 4 (February 23, 2007): 683–92, http://www.sciencedirect.com/science/article/pii/S0092867407001274.

CHAPTER SEVEN: INFORMATION INSCRIBED EVERYWHERE

1. Nicholas Wade "From One Genome, Many Types of Cells. But How?" *New York Times*, February 23, 2009, http://www.nytimes.com/2009/02/24/science/24chromatin.html.
2. Ibid.
3. In his opening paragraph, Wade writes: "Somehow each of the 200 different kinds of cells in the human body . . . must be reading off a different set of instructions written into the DNA." (Ibid.) By using the prepositional phrase "into the DNA," Wade means that each cell reads from a different subset of instructions. The context makes this clear. We have reworded Wade's "into the DNA" as "above and beyond" the DNA, because the markers that tell each cell which script lines to read (and which ones are off limits) are not themselves part of the DNA script.
4. Wade, "From One Genome."
5. Jonathan Wells's as-yet-unpublished paper is called "Designing an Embryo: Beyond Neo-Darwinism and Self-Organization." It may eventually be published as part of the proceedings of a symposium of more than a dozen scholars.

CHAPTER EIGHT: THE ZYGOTE VOYAGE

1. Stephen F. Ng and Joseph Frankel, "180 degree rotation of ciliary rows and its morphogenetic implications in *Tetrahymena pyriformis*," *Proceedings of the National Academy of Sciences of the United States of America* 74, no. 3 (March 1977): 1115–19, http://www.pnas.org/content/74/3/1115.full.pdf+html.
2. Richard Francis, *Epigenetics: The Ultimate Mystery of Inheritance* (New York: W.W. Norton, 2011), xiii.

CHAPTER NINE: THE EPIGENOME AND HUMAN HEALTH

1. "Epigenetics: Expert Q&A," NOVA Online, posted November 1, 2007, www.pbs.org/wgbh/nova/body/jirtle-epigenetics.html. The live Q&A sessions with Randy Jirtle ran on August 2 and November 1, 2007.

2. Jirtle cites published research from Dana C. Dolinoy, Dale Huang, and Randy Jirtle, "Maternal nutrient supplementation counteracts bisphenol A-induced DNA hypomethylation in early development," *Proceedings of the National Academy of Sciences of the United States of America* 104, no. 32 (August 7, 2007): 13056–61, http://www.pnas.org /content/104/32/13056.full.pdf+html.

3. Jirtle quoted in Bob Weinhold, "Epigenetics: The Science of Change," *Environmental Health Perspectives* 114, no. 3, http://dx.doi.org/10.1289 /ehp.114-a160 (accessed August 31, 2011). For a fascinating account of Jirtle's research, see the summary in the print edition of John Cloud, "Why Your DNA Isn't Your Destiny," *Time*, January 6, 2010, 50.

4. "Epigenetics: Expert Q&A."

5. Ibid. Jirtle cites published research from Ian C. G. Weaver et al., "Epigenetic programming by maternal behavior," *Nature Neuroscience* 7, no. 8 (August 2004): 847–54, http://www.nature.com/neuro/journal /v7/n8/full/nn1276.html. For histone deacetylases, Jirtle cites published research from Ian C. G. Weaver, Michael J. Meaney, and Moshe Szyf, "Maternal care effects on the hippocampal transcriptome and anxiety-mediated behaviors in the offspring that are reversible in adulthood," *Proceedings of the National Academy of Sciences of the United States of America* 103, no. 9 (February 28, 2006): 3480–85, http://www.pnas.org /content/103/9/3480.full.pdf+html.

6. "Epigenetics: Expert Q&A."

7. Ibid.

8. "Learning Without Learning," *Economist*, September 21, 2006, http:// www.economist.com/node/7941685.

9. Admittedly, the mechanics of how the epigenetic changes were triggered by the grooming and nurturing behavior is a bit complex; but these processes, along with a powerful biological trigger—a protein

called NGFI-A—are nicely summarized in the article, which can be read online at http://www.economist.com/node/7941685.

10. "Learning Without Learning."

11. "Acute Stress Leaves Epigenetic Marks on the Hippocampus," *Newswire,* Rockefeller University, November 23, 2009, http://newswire.rockefeller .edu/?id=1002&page=engine.

12. Ibid.

13. Ibid.

14. Christen Brownlee, "Chronic Stress May Cause Long-Lasting Changes," *JHU Gazette,* October 25, 2010, http://gazette.jhu.edu/2010/10/25/ chronic-stress-may-cause-long-lasting-changes.

15. Ibid.

16. Harrison Wein, "Stress Hormone Causes Epigenetic Changes," *NIH Research Matters,* September 27, 2010, http://www.nih.gov/research matters/september2010/09272010stress.htm.

17. Brownlee, "Chronic Stress May Cause Long-lasting Changes."

18. Ibid.

CHAPTER TEN: SPIRITUAL AND SOCIAL HEALTH

1. Matthew Parris, "As an Atheist, I Truly Believe Africa Needs God," *The Times* (London), December 27, 2008, http://www.timesonline.co.uk/ tol/comment/columnists/matthew_parris/article5400568.ece.

2. Byron R. Johnson, David B. Larson, and Timothy G. Pitts, "Religious Programs, Institutional Adjustment, and Recidivism among Former Inmates in Prison Fellowship Programs," *Justice Quarterly* 14, no. 1 (March 1997): 145–66; Byron R. Johnson and David B. Larson, "Linking Religion to the Mental and Physical Health of Inmates: A Literature Review and Research Note," *American Jails* 11, no. 4 (Sept/Oct 1997): 28–36; Byron R. Johnson, Sung Joon Jang, and Christopher Bader, "The Cumulative Advantage of Religiosity in Preventing Drug Use," *Journal of Drug Issues* 38, no. 3 (July 2008): 771–98.

3. To view selected portions of the Princeton study, see the "Princeton Chronicles" link at www.apologetics.org. Also, this video series,

published in 1995 by The Christian Network, and coproduced by the C. S. Lewis Society, is available in three half-hour segments. For more information, contact Dr. Thomas Woodward, 2430 Welbilt Blvd., Trinity, FL 34655.

4. Here we would simply invite anyone interested in the evidence for a biblical identification of the designer to visit apologetics.org, where several key articles are listed on the home page. For a printed overview of these issues, please request the free brochure "From Design to the Designer" from the C. S. Lewis Society, 2430 Welbilt Blvd., Trinity, FL 34655.

5. Michael Behe's numerous and detailed responses to his critics, after the June 2007 publication of *The Edge of Evolution*, are found on his blog, http://behe.uncommondescent.com/.

6. Noam Lahav, *Biogenesis: Theories of Life's Origin* (Oxford: Oxford University Press, 1999), 302.

7. For a more detailed tour of evidence pertaining to the design of the universe, see *The Privileged Planet* (both the book and DVD by the same name), and a pair of books authored by Oxford professor of mathematics John Lennox: *God's Undertaker* and *God and Stephen Hawking: Whose Design Is It Anyway?*

8. For more information about the remarkable meeting in Altenberg, Austria, see John Whitfield, "Biological theory: Postmodern evolution?" *Nature* 455 (September 11, 2008): 281–84; published online by Nature News, September 17, 2008, http://www.nature.com/news/2008/080917/full/455281a.html. See also, Gerd. B. Müller and Stewart A. Newman, eds., *Origination of Organismal Form* (MIT Press, 2003) and Massimo Pigliucci and Gerd B. Müller, eds., *Evolution—the Extended Synthesis* (MIT Press, 2010).

9. Richard Dawkins, *The Blind Watchmaker* (New York: W.W. Norton, 1986), 1.

CHAPTER ELEVEN: AN INFINITELY MORE COMPLEX GENOME

1. Erica Check Hayden, "Human Genome at Ten: Life Is Complicated," *Nature* 464 (April 1, 2010): 664–67; published online by Nature News,

Notes

March 31, 2010, http://www.nature.com/news/2010/100331/full/46466
4a.html.

2. See "'Genomic Junk' Is Cell's Air-Traffic Control," *Creation-Evolution Headlines*, July 20, 2009, http://creationsafaris.com/crev200907.htm.

3. Quoted in "New Roles Emerge for Non-Coding RNAs in Directing Embryonic Development," *ScienceDaily*, August 28, 2011, http://www.sciencedaily.com/releases/2011/08/110828141048.htm.

4. Evolutionary biologist Richard Sternberg, in a conference presentation in Dallas, Texas, December 2008.

5. Wen-Yu Chung et al., "A First Look at ARFome: Dual-Coding Genes in Mammalian Genomes," *PLoS Computational Biology* 3, no. 5 (May 18, 2007), http://www.ploscompbiol.org/article/info:doi/10.1371/journal.pcbi.0030091. Here is an excerpt from the article's abstract:

> Coding of multiple proteins by overlapping reading frames is not a feature one would associate with eukaryotic genes. Indeed, codependency between codons of overlapping protein-coding regions imposes a unique set of evolutionary constraints, making it a costly arrangement. Yet in cases of tightly coexpressed interacting proteins, dual coding may be advantageous. Here we show that although dual coding is nearly impossible by chance, a number of human transcripts contain overlapping coding regions. Using newly developed statistical techniques, we identified 40 candidate genes with evolutionarily conserved overlapping coding regions. Because our approach is conservative, we expect mammals to possess more dual-coding genes. Our results emphasize that the skepticism surrounding eukaryotic dual coding is unwarranted: rather than being artifacts, overlapping reading frames are often hallmarks of fascinating biology.

6. Gary Taubes, "The Sea Change That's Challenging Biology's Central Dogma," *Discover*, October 2009, http://discovermagazine.com/2009/oct/03-sea-change-challenging-biology.s-central-dogma.

7. Sidebar material adapted from "The RNA Code: Pseudogenes Functional, Help Prevent Cancer," Creation-Evolution Headlines, June 24, 1020, used by permission; http://crev.info/content/the_rna_code_pseudogenes_functional_help_prevent_cancer. "The RNA Code" cites the following sources: Laura Poliseno et al., "A Coding-Independent Function of Gene and Pseudogene mRNAs Regulates Tumour Biology," *Nature* 465 (June 24, 2010): 1033–38, doi: 10.1038/nature09144; Isidore Rigoutsos and Frank Furnari, "Gene-Expression Forum: Decoy for microRNAs," *Nature* 465 (June 24, 2010): 1016–17, doi: 10.1038/4651016a.

8. Cristina Luiggi, "Genome Blossoms," *Scientist* 24, no. 11 (November 1, 2010): 29.

9. Ibid.

10. Eric Werner, "What makes us human? Or why aren't we mice?" PLoS Biology, May 27, 2009; http://www.plosbiology.org/annotation/listThread.action?inReplyTo=info%3Adoi%2F10.1371%2Fannotation%2F15134b58-7375-48e7-9553-42979b51bb5d&root=info%3Adoi%2F10.1371%2Fannotation%2F15134b58-7375-48e7-9553-42979b51bb5d.

CONCLUSION

1. "Scientists Map Epigenome of Human Stem Cells During Development," *ScienceDaily*, February 4, 2010, emphasis added, http://www.sciencedaily.com/releases/2010/02/100203141326.htm.

2. Richard Swenson, *More Than Meets the Eye: Fascinating Glimpses of God's Power and Design* (Colorado Springs: NavPress, 2000), 17.

3. These ideas are found in many of Fuller's books, especially those that probe the intelligent design controversy. See, for example, *Dissent over Descent* (London: Icon, 2008).

4. See, for example, Isaiah 53:1–12 and Zechariah 12:10 in the Old Testament. In the New Testament, we find the same theme of redemption spoken of in 1 Peter 2:24 and 3:18, as well as Ephesians 2:8–10, Titus 3:5–8, and Acts 15:9–11. See our explanation of this data in "Redemption Explained" on the apologetics.org home page.

ACKNOWLEDGMENTS

We wish to thank the many people whose help in research, reflection, and editing made this book possible. Special thanks go to Gary Carter of St. Luke's Cataract and Laser Institute; to Joseph Condeelis, for his amazing visual illustrations; and to Dennis Hillman and the editors at Kregel Publications. We thank our wives for their great patience and encouragement throughout the process. We also wish to acknowledge the scientific review and counsel of many biologists and geneticists, including Dr. Jonathan Wells and Dr. Ralph Seelke, without whose guidance this book would not have been possible. Lastly, we thank the many biological researchers and experts on the epigenome—whose names we are not at liberty to mention due to the point of view of this book—sympathetic to intelligent design theory. May the day come soon when these questions of biological origins can be discussed with the calmness, clarity, and rhetorical balance they deserve.

ABOUT THE AUTHORS

DR. JAMES P. GILLS, who originated this project, is an ophthalmologist, a pioneer in cataract surgery, and founder of St. Luke's Cataract and Laser Institute in the Tampa Bay area (www.stlukeseye.com). He completed his MD at Duke University and his residency at Johns Hopkins University. In addition to writing books on medical topics such as astigmatism, Dr. Gills has become a researcher, lecturer, and author on the Darwin/design controversy, as well as a variety of other topics. Information about Dr. Gills's books can be found at http://lovepress.com/books.htm. Love Press, his nonprofit publishing ministry, has distributed more than eight million copies of his books as gifts to his patients and to the U.S. inmate population in over two thousand jails and prisons in all fifty states.

DR. THOMAS E. WOODWARD is research professor at Trinity College of Florida, teaching in the areas of the history of science and apologetics, and is the founder and director of the C. S. Lewis Society (www.apologetics. org). A graduate of Princeton University in history, he completed his doctorate at the University of South Florida in the rhetoric of science, a field of communication theory. His doctoral dissertation at the University of South Florida, "Aroused from Dogmatic Slumber," was published by Baker Books as *Doubts About Darwin: A History of Intelligent Design*. A sequel, *Darwin Strikes Back*, was released by Baker in 2006. Dr. Woodward has also been featured in an origins debate on CNBC's "Squawk Box" program.